Seasonality

Seasonality

A personal account of nature through the seasons

Ian Parsons

Whittles Publishing

Whittles Publishing Ltd,
Dunbeath,
Caithness, KW6 6EG,
Scotland, UK

www.whittlespublishing.com

ISBN 978-184995-505-8

Printed in the UK by Cambrian Printers Ltd

Contents

Acknowledgements

This book is a result of numerous discussions of mine with many people about the wildlife we see throughout the year, how it makes me feel, and how I think about it and the wider countryside. If you have ever listened patiently as I have yabbered on, then thank you! I would like to thank everybody throughout Britain that works, whether professionally or as a volunteer, to make this a far better country for wildlife than it otherwise would be.

I would like to thank Stuart Gillies and Pete Carr for generously allowing me to use a couple of their photos: much appreciated.

I would also like to thank Chris Sperring for bouncing his ideas off me as I bounce mine off him; it can be frustrating when you think no one is listening, but we will get there. And I look forward to meeting some of your whitebeams soon!

Thanks to all at Whittles Publishing for their support and their belief in me.

Finally, thanks to my wife Jo, whose constant support makes it all possible.

AUTHOR'S NOTE

I have given distances in the two ways we currently tend to express them in the UK; shorter distances in metric, longer in imperial, and for somewhere in the middle, both forms.

Introduction

The seasons of the year roll on regardless: an endless cycle that dictates the rhythm of life. Our lives used to be more led by the seasons than they are now and they held more significance for us; our superstitions, our activities, they were all guided by them. But now our lights and heating negate the darker nights and chill of the winter, and the supermarkets and their global suppliers mean that once-seasonal foods are now always available. The seasons may no longer seem so relevant to our daily activities, but even so the seasons do still play a part in all of our lives.

We look forward to spring and its metaphorical new start; we dream of summer holidays, soaking up the sun; we find that autumn brings a sense of natural harvest and woodland walks in among falling leaves; and then we have the festivities of the winter to look forward to. The role of the seasons in our own lives, although far more peripheral these days, is still there.

However, for the wildlife all around us seasons are everything. Spring, summer, autumn and winter are totalitarian authorities that rule their lives and govern their actions. It is the seasons and the accompanying lengthening and shortening of the daylight hours, as well as the rising and falling of the temperatures, that lay out the timetable for what happens in the natural world that we live in. The first blossom of blackthorn, the return of the swallow, the crisp bark of a roe buck in rut and the beautiful call of nocturnal redwings overhead: all of these are seasonal features.

Wildlife makes me tick. I still find it the same source of fascination that I did when I was a child, but with that sense of wonder and amazement there now comes something else. Watching wildlife, whether it is in my garden or out in the wider countryside, gives me an enormous sense of well-being. Quite simply, it makes me happy. Yes, we can and should look a bit deeper at our wildlife and the environment: by doing so we will see the problems that they both face and that humans still continue to cause; we mustn't lose focus of that. But in that moment of seeing something – in those few fleeting seconds when the spring sunshine reflects off the butter-yellow wings of the first brimstone butterfly of the year, or when the low winter sun dazzles back at us from the flashing under-wings of a tightly packed wader flock twisting and turning over the mudflats – that's when the pure enjoyment comes. The seasons can create magic moments for us all.

This is what this book is about. It is about the seasonality of our wildlife; it is about what we can see as the four seasons progress; it is about witnessing the changes that they bring to what is happening all around us. But above all it is a personal account of how wildlife and its seasonality makes me feel. I am writing this introduction as we progress towards what will be the end of the third national lockdown in Britain due to the coronavirus pandemic that has so drastically altered our own lives in the last twelve months. It has for most humans been a terrible year.

But it has also been a year that has opened our eyes to what wildlife can do to us, how it can lift our spirits, how it can help us to forget, even if just for a short while, everything else that is happening. Over these last twelve months we have come to realise that simple things like watching a blackbird flicking through our flower beds or observing a spider making its web in the corner of our windows can make us feel better. Nature is good for us. Nature can help us disconnect from our lives, from our troubles and thoughts that can otherwise gnaw away at us. By watching wildlife we can disconnect from all of that, and instead we can connect to whatever we are watching or listening to. Making that connection to wildlife or the environment around us helps us to re-engage with the seasons and it is also, I strongly believe, fundamental to our well-being.

The thoughts of seasonality in this book are my notes and observations of the wildlife I share my life with. I hope you can relate to them, and I hope that they may inspire you to watch the wildlife around you, whatever it may be, to form your own connections. It is written in a journal format, recording the wildlife as I saw it as the seasons progressed; sometimes the observations and happenings recorded link nicely into one another, at other times they don't. But that's a reflection of the wildlife around us; once you start looking, anything can happen! The following observations are primarily recorded in my home county of Devon, most based in and around my home village, nestled on its bend in a river on the mid-Devon plain just to the north of Dartmoor.

Virtually every species mentioned can be found right across the country. They are generally common, and you could therefore say that they are nothing special, but of course that would be wrong. They are all special, each and every one.

Ian Parsons
Devon

Spring

Beneath a clear, chill March sky, perched on a frost-cracked, time-eroded and lichen-encrusted mass of granite, I look out over the beginnings of the Taw river as it seeks its escape from the high ground of north Dartmoor. Alone, enjoying the ephemeral tranquillity of solitude, I sit on my hard seat watching distant scruffy sheep relentlessly browse the moorland flora. Here and there, wind-sculpted hawthorns, aeolian twisted tangles of resilience, break the monotony of openness.

I love this landscape. Dartmoor and its piles of granite have long been part of my life, a childhood playground, a place to explore and now a place to escape to. Above me a buzzard mews, the evocative call ringing in my ears as the moor grabs the bird's shadow, giving it a tangible life of its own as it races across the ground beneath me, the rough vegetation shackling the sun-cast image whilst the real thing reels in blue-sky freedom.

A small, tailed ball of brown skyrockets upward from the mosaic of grass, heather and gorse that surrounds the granite rocks I am sitting on. Up and up it goes until it becomes little more than a distant dot in the wide expanse of blue. And then its song rains down from high, soaking me in its beauty, a sound that signifies spring as well as an untamedness that has become increasingly rare in this modern world.

A bright blue sky, a rugged moorland landscape and a skylark singing: surely one of the most perfect of all combinations. The song of a skylark reaches out and touches us like few others can, a coalescence of pure notes invoking blue skies and carefree days; it is no wonder that these birds have inspired countless poets and composers over the generations. But these are not carefree days for the singing lark above me; his song is no more directed at me than it is at the unyielding igneous rock beneath me. He is singing to be heard, to be noticed – but not by me. These are perhaps the most important days of his short life.

This spring that is now dawning may be his only chance of breeding. The odds of him surviving to this time next year are slim; these small brown birds that bring such delight with their glorious song typically live for only two years.[1] Now is his time. Now he must

---

1 BTO BirdFacts, Skylark.

Skylarks abound on the high ground of north Dartmoor where the Taw River Marsh lies beneath the pointed hill of Steeperton Tor.

alert all others to his hold on this territory, his song both an attraction and a warning: a warning to other males that this piece of moorland belongs to him, and an attraction to females, informing them of his fitness for breeding, for rearing their young.

This grassy moorland in which I am sitting is prime skylark habitat. Modern farming has been unable to tame it as it has the old grassy hay meadows and spring-sown cereals of yesteryear. The intensification of farming in Britain has been catastrophic for the skylark since I was born; in the few decades of my existence, the population of skylarks in Britain has tumbled precipitously, by 75 per cent.[2] When I was a child the bird was a soundtrack to my adventures, accompanying me as I roamed the fields behind where we lived, seemingly always there, like the sun as I went on my Arcadian wanderings. I can remember craning my young neck as I tried to find the singer high up in the blue, trying to guess, as only a child can guess, how many miles it was above me. Childhood recollections of unending sunny days, ascending larks and their descending songs, indelible memories of an all too delible bird.

I come here often to this area of moorland, a semi-wild place where the skylarks still abound. The male above me is not alone; other distant dots are pouring out their song for all to hear, and up here it is easy to assume that all is well in the skylark's world. Dartmoor is not typical, though; it is a massive upswelling of granite, a place that the

Seasonality

2 Data taken from the Royal Society for the Protection of Birds website.

plough cannot break. I should be hearing them around my village, set in the very heart of bucolic Devon. I don't.

That is not strictly true: I have a favourite walk along some lanes that circumvent the village, over 3 miles (about 5 km) in length, and all of those 3 miles are through farmed countryside. At this time of year I can get a distant snatch of the laverock (as this small lark is sometimes known) singing just past the doctor's surgery, and then again where the lane passes a small local nature reserve, an SSSI of grassland, an island of wildlife value in a sea of intense management. The anthem of the lark should be throughout this walk – would have been throughout this walk just a few decades ago – but we have removed it in our myopic view of life.

It is not just the lark that has gone; many other farmland birds have also vanished from their old haunts, and they continue to disappear. When we first moved here just a handful of years ago, we would see three male yellowhammers, incandescent yellow burners proclaiming their territorial claims along the route. Now we see just the one.

But up here, up on the moor, on the high ground of its northern half, the exaltation of larks are performing a concerto of aural bliss. Their unending blend of rolling notes is all I can hear, enveloping me in sheer beauty, the song of poetic legend, tumbling from the blurred wing dots above. It makes me feel good to be alive.

There is an almost indescribable beauty to bird song; listening to the fluty notes of a blackbird or the elegiac outpourings of a robin is a pleasure you can lose yourself in, and it is important that we humans do so. Bird song is good for you: it is good for your mental health and your physical well-being, it reduces stress levels, it relaxes you and you don't need a prescription to indulge.[3] There is only one side-effect to this medicine: it is highly, highly addictive. My name is Ian and I am addicted to bird song.

The song and calls of birds are as varied as the birds themselves. Some are highly complex, others are simple: some are loud, demanding attention, others soft and quiet. There are barks and booms, whistles and clicks, whirling churrs and laughing chuckles, tumbling melodic notes and jarring shouts. Spring is the main season of song, the season to listen and enjoy, to lose yourself in wild melody. There is one song that I love to hear at this time of year. It is an evocative sound, full of meaning if not tune: it is the discordant two-syllable song of the chiffchaff – a thoroughly unworthy song in any other context, but in March it is an attention-grabbing herald of spring.

The two clashing notes of this small warbler announce its arrival back in its breeding territory as well as announcing that spring is here. There are many symbols of spring – you probably have your own – but it is the less than tuneful song of the chiffchaff that is

---

3 There have been numerous studies that have shown this: an example is 'Urban Mind: Using Smartphone Technologies to Investigate the impact of Nature on Mental Wellbeing in Real Time' *by Bakolis et al, BioScience, vol 68, issue 2, Feb 2018.*

mine. It is late morning on the last day of the weekend, and for the first time in a long time there is real warmth in the sunshine, a welcome sensation as I deadhead the already gone-over daffodils in the garden. And then I hear it: 'Chiff Chaff, Chiff Chaff'. The song stops my snipping and I stand up, smiling. I can't see the bird – the sound is coming from some trees and shrubs a few gardens over – but it doesn't matter. It is the song, the dissonant song, that matters. Spring is here.

This small unobtrusive, some might even say drab, warbler may have returned from southern Europe or even Africa, but it could also be one of the birds that have chanced their arm, gambled on our changing climate and chosen to see out the winter here. In recent years more and more chiffchaffs have overwintered in Britain, surviving through the colder weather, gleaning enough food to sustain themselves, keeping their peace until the spring sunshine draws out their two-note song once more. These avian chancers are vulnerable to prolonged cold snaps, but the warming climate means that these are getting less likely, at least in the South West of the UK. It could be that these tiny migrants are already on the road to becoming partial residents.[4]

Bright butter-yellow wings flutter by, a vivid vibrancy in the warmth of the March sun. A male brimstone butterfly, like the chiffchaff a symbol of spring, immaculate in its appearance, flashes across the garden without pausing. Immaculate it may be, but this is no newly hatched adult; his sulphurous yellow wings made their debut in the world several months ago, during the sun-kissed warmth of last August. For most of his adult life he has kept his colour under wraps, sleeping through much of the autumn and all of the winter months, deep in hibernation, hidden in amongst the evergreen leaves of plants like ivy and holly, his folded wings subduing his colouration, giving him the look of an old withered leaf, rather than the beaming yellow delight that he has once more become.

The spring sun and its heat have woken him from his climate-induced slumber, and now he is on the move, full of life once more, in his delicate but determined flight to seek out breeding grounds and the females he will find there. Leaving the village and its ivy-clad outbuildings and walls, leaving the holly hedges and the thatched roofs, abandoning the multitude of hibernation sites, flying serenely over the people in their cars speeding through their lives below, heading for the snake of wet woodland down by the site of the old mill where the alder buckthorn grows. A native and widespread tree across much of the country, but a tree few people know, unobtrusive in size and habits, the alder buckthorn is a tree that slips under the radar of most. But the brimstone knows it; he would have munched his way through its oval green leaves last spring and summer, and now he seeks it again – but this time not for leaves; his only interest now is the females of his kind.

The alder buckthorn is one of many native trees and shrubs that are poorly known, and as I look around the garden I see another one, the guelder rose, a species of viburnum

---

4 As an example, at least 90 birds overwintered at a south Devon sewage farm, as reported in an article in *British Birds*, vol 113, March 2020.

The brimstone butterfly is a brilliant yellow announcement of the coming of spring. (Photo by kind permission of Peter James Carr Photography.)

whose bright red berries no doubt helped it get established here. The berries are a favoured food of many birds, and it is most likely they who unwittingly planted this specimen, carefully depositing the seed wrapped in the bird's very own specially provided compost. This will be this small tree's third spring; its leaves are not out yet, but the pointed buds on either side of the stems are beginning to enlarge, to swell with the promise of what is to come. Many of us are blind to trees – we see them, of course, but we don't see them as individual species, especially not the smaller types of tree that our countryside has in abundance. To us they become a homogenous twiggy mass; we don't see the tree for the trees. Wonderfully named trees such as the wayfaring tree and the spindle are common and beautiful; again they are natives, a natural part of our countryside, but like the alder buckthorn and the guelder rose they too are often overlooked.

These native trees are all part of the ecosystems around us; they provide sustenance and habitat for many species, some of which depend heavily on them. The beautiful black-speckled white spindle ermine moth needs the spindle tree just as the beautiful yellow brimstone butterfly needs the alder buckthorn. These insects cannot afford to be tree-blind, yet we often are when actually we should be following their example, opening our eyes a bit more, looking more closely at the fabulous species we have growing around us.

The pure white blossom of a blackthorn against a blue March sky.

One tree that is easily seen at this time of the year is the blackthorn. The beginning of March sees the still-drab hedgerows and road verges suddenly peppered with white blossom, bringing a welcome brightness to any journey. In some places the white is sporadic in its coverage, in others the coverage is akin to snow, a dazzling whiteness reflecting the sun on those rare blue-sky mornings. The blackthorn belongs to the Prunus genus, as do peaches, almonds and cherries, and the blackthorn too bears fruit later in the year, when its fruits, the sloes, ripen into a purple-sheened promise of decadent liqueurs on cold winter nights.

But for the blackthorn's fruits to come to fruition its beautiful snow-white blossoms need to be pollinated now, in March, and for that to happen the sun has to shine, to tempt forth the queen bumblebees from their winter slumbers. When they first emerge, these furry insects are almost spent. They are desperate to refuel on nectar, and the early-flowering blackthorn, whose blossoms come out before its leaves, provides the nectar- and pollen-rich flowers the bumblebees require. For the earliest emergers the flowers can help kick-start the new colonies. In March, blackthorns don't just look pretty; they are a vital part of the chain of life that surround us.

The blackthorn is a scruffy-looking tree when looked at through our eyes: a tangle of twisted, angular branches, armed with fierce spines as the second part of its scientific name suggests.[5] It spreads its way through hedgerows and woodland edges, ready to launch forth into open grassy spaces if allowed to do so by the mowers and grazers. It is a pioneer species, primed to begin the transformation of open habitats into woodland. Its tangled form and sharply pointed attitude have long been used by us to form impenetrable hedges and barriers. It is a common native tree, but it is not a conspicuous one – apart from at this time of year, that is, when its clean white flowers light up the sides of roads and paths, guiding us on the journey into spring.

On the margins

A tickle of a breeze ruffles the newly emerged leaves of the hawthorn, from within which a robin sings. A male blackbird replies with his own song from an imperious-looking ash tree, its normally graceful branches ending in the ephemeral flowers that give the tree a temporary knobbly look. As I peer down the slope I can see the large leaves of sycamore unfolding themselves, their dormancy over; these maples rush to open their solar panels

The grey squirrel is a widespread and familiar mammal in many cities.

---

5 *Prunus spinosa*: the name literally means spiny plum.

and get their photosynthetic factories working again. A grey squirrel barks its strange alien call; it is easy to spot, sitting along a branch and rippling its long tail over its back as it calls loudly, emphasising its claim to the immediate area. The squeaky bike-pump song of a great tit catches my attention; like the mammalian North American[6] colonist, it too is staking its claim. I soon spot it and its mate; they are scouring the old stone retaining wall a bit further along the path. At first I think they are looking for food, searching for spiders and the like tucked into the many crevices and cracks. But it soon becomes obvious that they are looking for something else.

Great tits are very colourful birds: black and white heads, and that fantastic yellow front with its bold black stripe running down the middle. At first the males and females look alike to us, but if you look more closely you can soon learn to spot the difference. The black stripe that runs down their yellow front is the key: in females it is narrow and often broken, whereas in the male it is wider and continuous, and gets broader as it reaches the belly. I use this feature as I watch the pair in front of me exploring the wall; the male is interspersing his time on the stones with little sojourns up onto an overhanging branch from which he sings his characteristic two-note song. The female is giving the wall a far more thorough examination, focusing on the many holes in the ancient mortar lines; she squeezes herself through one of these holes and disappears into the inner recesses of the wall. The male flies down to the wall and looks around this small gap; as he does so, the female re-emerges – but not from the hole she had entered by: she shimmies herself out of another hole maybe 20 centimetres further along the mortar line. These birds aren't looking for food; they are prospecting for a nest site.

The female finds another hole, a bit higher up than the previous one, and a bit bigger too. She grips the outside of the wall on her delicate dark legs as she peers in, then she slips inside. The male hangs around the outside, occasionally hopping up onto the same branch as before; he seems full of nervous energy, constantly moving about. After what seems an age, but in reality was probably only about twenty seconds, the female re-emerges. The male flies down to the wall and watches her as she grips the hole entrance and once again looks inside. Satisfied, she flies up to the branch, quickly followed by her mate, who lands beside her and sings. I think they may have found a potential.

Great tits are hole nesters; we normally associate them with nesting in tree holes, not stone holes. However tree holes are often in short supply, especially here. There may be plenty of bird song and trees about me, but I am standing in the centre of the city of Exeter, on the boundary of where a formal city centre parks drops downwards to meet the railway line below. The park is neatly and formally managed, and the railway line itself is kept clear of any potential untidiness, but the margin of land on the steep slope between the two has been left to look after itself. And it is here that the leaves are bursting forth from their buds, it is here that the squirrel is setting up territory, and it is here that the birds are singing and looking for nest sites. This steep, inaccessible part of the city is wild, a no man's land for humans.

---

6 The grey squirrel was introduced to Britain in the 1870s.

Seasonality

8

From the hole-nesting great tit's point of view, the sycamore-dominated woodland that has sprung up along the slope is a great food source, but the young age of the trees means there aren't many, if any, tree holes in which they can nest. Trees take time to develop dead wood and holes, and these trees are still in the vigour of their youth. The grey squirrel and its kin are doing their best to accelerate the ageing process, stripping the thin, smooth bark of the sycamores, creating dead wood and swelling scar tissue, all of which has the potential to develop further, to create nest holes – but that is still some years into the future. There is, however, a food source to be exploited, and the great tits are prepared to be flexible in order to do so. A nest in a hole in a stone wall may not be typical, but it will certainly do.

The return of a favourite

Spring marches into April, and the month announces itself with a spell of rain, but this year instead of the fabled showers it is steady, persistent rain. Eventually the clouds wear themselves out and begin to dissipate; a high-pressure system locks onto the weather map and as it does so it brings a returning favourite. Making their graceful arcs across the blue sky, the aerial elegance of swallows in flight is as distinctive as it is delightful. The first swallows of the year have arrived, cutting through the air in a flurry of fast wing beats and serene glides. The song of the chiffchaff may be the sound that signifies

The beautiful swallow; its return to our skies in the spring is always a welcome sight.

spring for me, but it is the swallow that is the visual indicator. They are brilliant birds, beautiful delicate flyers. But don't let their delicacy of flight deceive you; these are long-distance migrants, spanning the globe as they follow the long hours of daylight across the hemispheres. These are birds that don't know what mid-winter is.

The beauty of these birds and the fact that they will often nest in close proximity to us means that the swallow has long been a bird of fascination. Early naturalists debated among themselves the significance of the bird's sudden springtime appearance after months of absence. Where the birds went to for the winter months was a mystery: there was talk of hibernation, even metamorphosis, but slowly the understanding of the principle of migration dawned. Swallows disappeared in the autumn and returned in the spring because they went elsewhere in the world to live.[7]

Our swallow, the barn swallow, is a prodigious migrant, and in 1912 it was finally confirmed just how far these small birds, weighing in at around 20 grams, will actually go in their pursuit of the sun. A bird that had been ringed in northern England was subsequently recovered in the Natal area of South Africa, 6,000 miles away.[8] In other words, these small graceful flyers are racking up around 12,000 miles a year in migration flights alone.

Spending your life in perpetual spring and summer may sound idyllic, but the reality of migration is a hard, unforgiving one. Of the myriad of young swallows that gathered on the phone and electric cables spanning the village streets last autumn, it is likely that only one in every five of them has survived long enough to have made it back this spring to breed. The swallow above me – a blur of iridescent wings pursued by long tail streamers – is one of the lucky ones; but even though its journey is over the bird is still at risk. Another low pressure barrelling in off the Atlantic or a sudden cold snap will make it difficult for this new arrival to find food, and without food it will quickly lose condition and perish. Nature is always on the edge, and for the insect-eating traveller above me that edge is particularly sharp.

I watch the new arrival for several minutes. It seems to revel in the airspace above the village, sometimes dashing in pursuit of a small parcel of protein-packed fly, at other times leisurely floating in ever-increasing circles, wafting through the air rather than flying. I marvel at its journey, thinking of the jungle, the savannah, the Sahara, the open sea that this bird has crossed to get to Europe – and then, not satisfied with that, it kept on going, heading further north, crossing forests and agricultural land, skirting around mountain ranges, skimming past cities and estuaries, crossing yet more open inhospitable stretches of sea, before rising over the cliffs of south Devon and heading for the village in which I stand now, watching this tough, beautiful survivor. I am grinning broadly. I can't help it – this first swallow might not have made the summer, but it has certainly made my day.

---

7 For an example of these early thoughts see *The Natural History of Selbourne*, Gilbert White, 1789.

8 *The Migration Atlas: Movements of the Birds of Britain and Ireland*, Chris Wernham et al, Poyser, 2002.

Busy spring garden

Distrustful dunnocks follow each other across the garden, relentlessly bound to their innate breeding strategy of doubt. House sparrows call noisily from the thatch above, busy ransacking it for nesting materials, whilst a wren boisterously sings its loud tune from within the leafing branches of the hawthorn.

Suddenly the song and calls stop, the sparrows dive headlong into the honeysuckle-bramble tangle, a blackbird explodes in noisy panic, the dunnocks recklessly rocket into the vertical ivy forest that clads the old stone wall. A male sparrowhawk – flying terror for the small birds, beautiful barred vision for me – glides by overhead, not stopping, leaving fear in its wake. Only the wren makes a sound: a harsh, scolding, repetitive tick.

The king of birds[9] is the first to stand down from the accipiter-imposed state of trepidation. Appearing on the top of the wall, tail cocked, legs dipped, it rips out the song from within, a stentorian blast of incredible volume, taking advantage of the other birds' continued reluctance. Satisfied, it drops down to the pots on the patio, scurrying between them, investigating everything, then the wren switches from bird to mouse, disappearing into the tight spaces between the pots, even slipping underneath the larger ones, supported as they are on small pottery feet.

With the mouselike behaviour of the wren, so the other birds begin to emerge from the cover. The verbose sparrows are typically first: hesitant to begin with, they soon forget the predator and revert to their more usual noisy gregarious behaviour. A dunnock drops down out of the ivy, followed two seconds later by a second. They look identical to me, but their behaviour allows me to make an informed judgement as to the sex of the two. The first bird is likely to be the female and the dedicated follower the male, keen to tail his mate to try and prevent her meeting other males, a strategy that will inevitably fail.

Dunnocks are notoriously not monogamous: a brood of dunnock chicks huddled together in their nest are going to be the offspring of more than one male. The relationships between the males and the females of this otherwise unassuming bird are pure soap opera drama. The male will try to persuade his mate to be faithful by scouring the area for food, food which he can then feed to her to prove his qualities. But when he is searching for food he is unable to follow her closely, allowing her the freedom to meet other nearby males. In any case, his search for sustenance may well also lead him to another female, and so the social web of dunnock life grows ever more complicated. Dunnocks may have, at least to our eyes, a somewhat complicated breeding strategy, but it is a strategy that works for them.

As I watch these two capricious birds, my eye is caught by a semaphore message from the fresh leaves of the clematis that straggles, but not struggles, up through the ivy. A male orange-tip butterfly, my first of the year, flashes its eponymous wingtips once more

---

9 According to folklore the wren is the king of birds. The story goes that the birds had a competition to find their king, and it was decided that the bird that could fly the highest would be the winner. The eagle outflew all the other birds, but unknown to this raptor a wren had hidden away in its plumage, and as the eagle reached the peak of its climb, the wren popped out and, flying a little higher still, claimed the title.

before dashing upwards to chase another butterfly that to me is just an unidentifiable silhouette against the bright sky. Early April orange-tips, newly emerged from their chrysalis in which they performed their metamorphtastic[10] change, are regulars in our garden, using the Jack by the hedge[11] that grows with rampant freedom to carefully deposit its eggs on. But they don't lay their eggs in batches: they lay them one at a time, one egg per flower head, and if they should discover another orange-tip has already laid on the plant they will move on to seek flower heads that are free from eggs.

The female butterflies are cautious for good reason. The caterpillars of the orange-tip feed on members of the cabbage family, particularly cow parsley and the aforementioned Jack by the hedge, but they will also forsake their vegetarian diet if the opportunity arises, feeding on each other should a female get careless in her egg-laying and deposit one of her small eggs too close to another one. There are cannibals in the garden.

A blue tit appears. Distracting me from mental images of rapacious caterpillars, it drops down into the smoke bush before flicking upwards with acrobatic ease and landing on the face of the bird box attached to the side of the steps that connect the upper part of the garden to the lower. It pops its white-cheeked head briefly inside the small-diameter hole, looks around the outside with a knowing eye and then hops up onto the top of the box. It appears to examine the wooden roof thoroughly before flying up into the untidy mass of hawthorn branches above.

It is a new box. I made it last year and put it up at the beginning of December, an addition to the other boxes already placed in various parts of the garden. The prospecting blue tit is a good sign, and a welcome one. The joy you can get from having birds decide to rear their brood in your own box in your own garden is immense, and with this box just a few metres from the kitchen window, my fingers are most definitely crossed that it will get used. These small colourful avian gymnasts might have some competition, though; in the last week I have seen a male house sparrow pay attention to the entrance hole, eyeing it carefully. The hole's diameter is small enough to deter sparrows, but another bird has been checking it out as well. At the end of March a nuthatch visited the box on several occasions, and whilst the hole might be too small for them, nuthatches, unlike sparrows, have the perfect tool to enlarge it so that it meets their requirements.

The dagger-like bill of these tree-trunk runners is the perfect chisel for enlarging the entrance, evolved to literally hatchet nuts in two; the soft pine timber of the box will not present much of a challenge for it. But the nuthatch, although calling loudly nearby and frequently charging headlong on to the bird table, scattering seeds and birds before it, hasn't revisited the box for at least a week. Perhaps it has found another site, and if so the blue tit may well be able to lay claim to the box for itself. As if to confirm this, about thirty minutes after I first saw it scrutinise the box, the tit returned, this time not alone. A second blue tit watched it carefully from the hawthorn as it again landed on the front of the box and peered into its recesses. After the first completed its survey it flew up to

---

10 My portmanteau: metamorphous + fantastic.
11 Also known as garlic mustard, *Alliaria petiolata*.

join the second, and the two of them progressed through the branches, searching for and finding food before moving off out of sight. I am hoping they will return for a full viewing soon.

For me, spring is full of rediscovery and reacquaintance; it is about the pleasure of re-learning bird song unheard for many months, discerning the graceful, balletic flight of the returning hirundines, remembering wild flowers as they pop up for their time in the sun, and saying hello to old friends in the garden, amphibious dragon-like friends. The newts are suddenly much more visible in our pond. I watched one earlier as it materialised out of the depths, coming up to the surface and snatching some air before heading back down into the darkness. They have been back for a few weeks, but they are easy to overlook in the darkness of the pond. The spring sun raising the temperature of the days will have warmed them as they slept in their winter quarters, safely tucked away somewhere in the garden, and roused them back into activity. We have a good population of palmate newts using our pond; they are our smallest newt species,[12] measuring only 8 centimetres in length. They are beautiful creatures, intricately marked on their back and sides with a speckled pattern of dark green randomly layered over a background of lighter, more olive, green. On the underside, their bellies are orange, and the males have several dark brown spots scattered across this orange whilst the females have only a few or even none at all. They have very pale throats and these are clear of spots – a good, if not wholly reliable, way of distinguishing them from the very similar smooth newt that so far I haven't recorded using our pond.

Now that they are back in the water they can turn their attention to breeding; the males chase the females through their three-dimensional liquid world, cutting them off and barring their way before performing their display in front of them, curling their tail around their bodies and vibrating it rapidly. If the female is receptive she will watch the male perform; if not she will simply swim off, leaving the male to his tail-shaking. They lay their eggs in amongst the pond's aquatic vegetation, and it is only a couple of weeks or so before these hatch into small tadpole-like larvae that soon develop legs and gradually become more newt-like over the next couple of months.

We get frogs in the pond pretty much all year around, poking their heads up out of the water to watch us as we watch them; there are usually about five or six of them using it as a refuge in the day before venturing out around the garden to assist us with our organic slug control at night. It is only when it turns really cold in the winter months that you notice their absence, but given a bit of new year sunshine those heads will be back watching all around them. Now that April is with us I would expect to see lots of black tadpoles sunning themselves on the shallow pond-lined slope, but this year there are no more than a handful to be found.

The reason for this lack of tadpoles is there in plain sight. The pond's dragons may

12 *The British Amphibians and Reptiles*, Malcolm Smith, New Naturalist Series, 1951.

We might not think it, but newts are voracious predators of frog spawn.

be small, but they are fearsome predators of frogspawn and young tadpoles, picking them off with ease. Having a good pond for newts comes with a price, a price that the frogs pay. In late February, I went out to the pond after darkness had fallen, and with my torch I highlighted a clump of newly deposited frogspawn, the jelly-like structure looking almost ethereal in the artificial light. But also highlighted by my torch were four newts: three of them were browsing the outer edge of the jellied mass and the other one had plunged its head and forelimbs right in. They were all feeding on the frogspawn and they continued to feed despite my torchlight. It is an amphibian-eat-amphibian world out there.

Our pond supports good numbers of newts, which means that it is heavily compromised as a breeding pond for frogs. The newts exact a heavy toll, but the frog's breeding strategy is a numbers game. An average clump of spawn will have anywhere between 1,000 and 2,000 eggs[13] within it, so despite the heavy predation some of these eggs will hatch; some of the newly hatched tadpoles will escape the continued onslaught, and then as they get bigger they also get more elusive and difficult for the newts to snatch.

13 Data taken from Froglife website, www.froglife.org .

Garden ponds are brilliant things, a must-have for any wildlife gardener; as they bring a whole new dimension to the species your garden can support. Ponds don't have to be big, they don't have to be deep; put one in and the wildlife will soon find it. Ponds support dragonflies, whirling beetles, dragon-like newts and nosy frogs – all you have to do is add water.

An evening by the sea

Crunching across a pebble beach in the early evening sunlight, we pass a couple of fishermen ensconced in their fold-up chairs next to their angled rods that point far out to sea, and we walk on for another hundred yards or so before deciding, for no particular reason, that this patch of smooth rounded pebbles where we are standing is perfect. Sitting atop one of the shelved ridges that run in parallel lines along the arcing beach, we stare out at the mesmerising sea before us.

Behind us, the pebble-strewn red cliffs of Devon's Jurassic coast tower upwards, cutting us off from the human-dominated world beyond. In front of us is the sea, shimmering in the lowering sunlight, flat calm with just a hint of movement, captivating us with its tranquil beauty. Two cormorants are flying low over the water, a combination of fast wing beats and sticking-out necks. They pass a shag heading whence they came, the smaller size of their green-glossed relative evident as their paths cross.

A herring gull, flying along the water line with deliberate deep wingbeats as it scours the lapping waters, diverts inland a fraction, changing its flight path to fly right over us, staring intently as it passes, assessing our potential as food providers, but correctly

The great black-backed gull dwarfs the more familiar herring gull. The fearsome bill of the larger bird belies its predatory nature.

deciding that the bundled mass of stranded seaweed further along the beach offers more of an opportunity. A raptorial great black-backed gull glides on its white-fringed black wings over the open water; these are fearsome marine predators, pirates if you like, capable of chasing down and killing a wide variety of birds and mammals, but this bird is in serene mode, its impressive wingspan keeping it aloft as it sails above the sea.

With the binoculars I spot a long-winged white bird way out from shore; as I watch, it suddenly folds up its wings, revealing the black towards their ends, and plummets downwards, crashing head on with the sea below. Gannet! Pure dive-bombing exhilaration, smashing through the glassy ocean surface in pursuit of its fishy prey. Even at this distance I am able to clearly witness the transformation from long-winged seabird shape to the ultra-streamlined missile it becomes just before it arrows into the water.

As gannets enter the watery world of the sea they can be doing in excess of 60 miles an hour. The potential for injury at those speeds is high; impacting the relatively dense medium of sea water can hurt, badly. But gannets don't hit the water, they pierce it. Everything about their body shape as they enter the water is perfectly streamlined; they are avian bullets, shooting through the surface, their dives continuing onwards for up to eleven watery metres. The fish are sitting ducks.

The gannets soon move on, full of fish and heading back to their nesting colony on a towering cliff. The birds that we have just been watching are probably breeding off the Brittany coast, a short commute over open water for these efficient fishers and flyers.

For some minutes, a jet-black carrion crow has been waddling along the pebbles, heading in our general direction, and pausing its waddling to examine anything of interest it comes across, or to check on us with its beady eye, ensuring that we pose it no threat. It has been a laid-back meandering along the stones, but as we watch it, enjoying its amusing gait, the bird suddenly becomes very alert. It stops moving and stares intently upwards. Its change in behaviour is our cue and we take it, swivelling around on ourselves, looking upwards into the sky. We immediately see the crow's concern.

A peregrine, the sun picking out the white of the bird's throat which in turn emphasises the menacing executioner's hood of a head. The powerful, speed record-holding hunter is flying along the clifftop. But its pace is leisurely and there is no intent; even so the crow watches warily as the predator passes. The falcon's flight on shallow beats takes it back over the skyline of red, crumbling Jurassic cliff. The crow watches for a few moments more before hopping rapidly towards the cliff base; it is much more edgy now, its relaxed beachcombing forgotten, and after a quick look around it takes to the air, shouting out its displeasure as it does so. It flies on busy wings, keeping close to the cliff face, flying fast along it in the opposite direction to the one the falcon took.

We turn our attention back to the sea. The evening light reflects back off the smooth, untroubled waters, some far-off gulls flash white at us, lit up by the sun, pearl-like travellers across the blue as they flap their unhurried way along, whilst another cormorant travels low beneath them over the serene surface. The water gently laps against the smooth pebbles, a relaxing sound to a relaxing view. Everybody needs to sit by the sea.

No Parking here

I see it clearly, far clearer than the hazy outline of Wales on the horizon. My companions and I can all make out Wales on the far side of the Bristol Channel, but it's just me that sees what's lying much closer to us, just a few metres away at the point where the close-cropped grass meets the bracken edge. In amongst the broken remains of last year's stems and fronds, amidst the small fresh knobs of ferny growth that are already poking through the litter of last year, there lies a completely still male adder, basking in the sunshine. Adders are stunning creatures, beautiful patterned reptiles that for many blend seamlessly into the background of the habitat in which they are found. I would wager that many of you reading this will have at least once in your life walked right past a basking adder without ever being aware it was there.

It is easy to understand how you could miss them; they are beautifully camouflaged. Their colouration has evolved over countless generations, allowing them to be both predator and protected, to lie unseen in ambush and undetected in hiding. But the incongruity of my own colour blindness means that to me they are very visible indeed. They don't leap out at me, I don't see them as a glowing luminous entity; they are just there, visible to my eyes, their camouflage failing to deceive me.

I point out the basking male to my companions, but from where we stand none of them can see it; their vision is tricked by the snake's procryptic patternation. They might not be able to see it, but my mentioning of this hidden viper has caused a reaction; they have all become nervous at the thought that a snake is nearby. The idea of me taking them closer to it to show them is, apparently, not a good one. Instead we walk briskly past, with just me able to see him tasting the air with his fast tongue, staring out unblinking with fierce-looking eyes as we move onwards towards the cliffs, each one but me now sticking steadfastly to the centre of the surfaced path. I feel slightly disappointed that they don't share my joy in seeing this amazing predator, but I am not surprised.

Snakes trouble the human psyche. The slithering image is not a good one, especially when combined with venomous fangs – and yes, some species can be a real danger in many parts of the world. But not here, on the North Devon Coast Path. Britain has only three native species of snake: the widespread grass snake, the less widespread adder, and the rare smooth snake. The grass snake and the smooth snake are regarded as being non-venomous as they do not deliver venom via fangs,[14] but the adder is very much a venomous viper. Its bite is said to be very painful, but it is generally not considered

---

14 It has recently been proposed that many more snakes are technically venomous, even those that don't possess fangs to deliver it. Venom, as we generally think of it, is modified saliva that is injected into another animal via a bite. But it is possible that the saliva of snakes that don't bite, and are therefore widely considered as non-venomous, may indeed be toxic to some degree.

dangerous unless the receiver of the bite has a pre-existing condition that renders them vulnerable to it. The last known death due to an adder bite in Britain was in 1975, and to put that into perspective statistics tell us that five people every year die in Britain due to insect stings.[15]

The male adder I have just seen was coiled around itself, the diagnostic dark zig-zag pattern clear to see, to my eyes at least, against the almost silvery-grey background of the body, a body flattened against the ground to maximise the snake's surface area exposed to the all-important reptile energy source that is the sun. This flattening of the body can trick the eye into thinking that the snake that you are looking at is much bigger than it really is, but adders don't generally measure more than 60 to 70 centimetres in length, with adders measuring over 61 centimetres (2 feet) considered to be large examples.[16]

The path goes around the corner, and the county of Devon abruptly stops in front of us. The land drops precipitously down the towering rocky cliff to the sea below. There is no graduation: the land is there and then it is not. Far below us in the swelling sea a raft of razorbills bob up and down like black and white corks, and further out a few gulls dot the surface of the brooding grey water. Closer to, a buzzard is surfing the flow of air as it pushes up the cliff face, its broad wings fully open as it rides the current, using it to follow a course along the steep inaccessible faces with the minimum of effort. My friends stand close to the edge, leaning out recklessly over the sheer drop to look at where the waves crash against the rock far below – scared of unseen adders, but seemingly oblivious to the very visible danger right in front of them. We humans are odd creatures.

Later on we explore inland, following the course of a river in through its steep, wooded Exmoor valley. I want to show my friends a tree, but not just any tree. I want to show them a tree that is found nowhere else on this planet, I want to show them the No Parking whitebeam. Britain has very little in the way of endemic species – species that are only found naturally in the one place – but we do have a number of whitebeam species that are only found here in Britain, and the rugged, cleaved land of Exmoor is a place where at least five of these unique species are found.

One of these species is extremely limited in its range. The No Parking whitebeam is only found here, in the East Lyn valley; it is found nowhere else on Exmoor, nowhere else in Devon, nowhere else in the world. There are fewer than 200 of these trees in existence, and all of them are here, clinging on to the steep-sided terrain among the other trees, various ferns and an abundant coating of moss and lichen in the woodland that stands above the rushing, wild white waters of the East Lyn. It is a beautiful and evocative setting in which to meet such a special tree.

The one I am introducing to my companions is known as the type specimen; it was the tree that was first identified as being a bit different from all other trees, in particular the Devon whitebeam, a close relative and a tree relatively far more widespread throughout the county. This particular tree was first noted in the 1930s, growing by a small layby in

---

15 Statistical causes of death in the UK taken from the *Report on The Terrorism Acts in 2011* by David Anderson QC.
16 *The British Amphibians and Reptiles,* Malcolm Smith, New Naturalist Series, 1951.

The type specimen of the No Parking whitebeam tree that was first noticed in the 1930s as being a potentially new species. Now showing signs of age, it still stands beside the parking spot near Lynmouth, from whence the species got its common name.

the road that winds up through the valley. A note was made of the tree's appearance, the location recorded. It could easily be found again, as someone had nailed a sign on it, a sign that told all passers that no parking was allowed in the layby.

The sign had long vanished by the time the tree was finally recognised as being its own species in 2009, but the sign's legacy lives on in the tree's name: the No Parking whitebeam has to be one of the strangest names there is for a tree, but it's perfect for this one. The appropriate epithet is also used in its scientific name: *admonitor* is from the Latin, meaning 'someone who admonishes, tells off'; you can almost imagine the tree wagging a finger-like branch at any motorist who looks covetously at the space beneath it.

The tree is no impressive giant; it is just a tree growing beside a road. Today as we look at it we can see a bit of dieback in its crown, and it has aged in the sometimes inhospitable climate of Exmoor, but the buds have burst and new leaves have unfurled once again. The amazing thing about this tree is that there is absolutely no public recognition of it, there is nothing in the valley to tell you that this is the only place on earth where this tree grows. The valley is owned by a conservation charity, the public are invited, encouraged, onto the land, yet there is no announcement of the fact that here, and only here, this tree grows. If the tree was a flower, a mammal, a butterfly or a bird its uniqueness would be everywhere, and its image would be on all sorts of marketing materials, probably even road signs. But this tree, which gets its name from an old road sign, stands anonymously without any celebration.

To add insult to injury, there are two cars parked underneath it.

The box is claimed

Another beakful of moss makes its way across the patio to the nest box, but it doesn't go direct. It first pauses on the stones by the pond, before flying up to the ivy on the wall, then into the smoke bush, where it flits from branch to branch before suddenly dashing to the front of the box and disappearing inside. A few seconds later, the blue tit wiggles its way out of the hole at the front of the box and flies direct across the patio with alacrity, avoiding the circuitous path of the inward journey.

A few minutes later and the bird returns with yet more moss, innately taking the previous roundabout route, attempting to mislead any potential watching predator as to where the nest it's building is located. The box that was so eagerly prospected by the blue tits just a few weeks ago has evidently become their chosen location for the nest that is now being constructed. Sometimes the bird is in and out in seconds, whilst at other times it stays within for longer, arranging its delivery of moss, hooking the material together, slowly forming the cup in which the female will lay her brood of eggs. We watch the tit's constant activity with a sense of pride; our box has tenants, and the pleasure they bring us is more than enough to cover the rent.

Both birds are involved, so at times one of them has to wait on the top of the box whilst its mate is inside arranging the latest delivery. There is plenty of communication

Another beakful of moss makes its way into the bird box in the hawthorn.

between the two, with grating warning calls whenever another bird appears within the vicinity, but they seem unbothered by us watching them work. They decide to take a break, to seek sustenance, but they don't travel far, always remaining in view of the box as they glean the branches of the hawthorn for food, probing the base of the flower clusters, checking the underside of the leaves, constantly moving, one minute hanging upside down, the next hopping along a side shoot.

A great tit flies into the tree, perching about a metre up from the box. It is greeted with an instant chorus of angst from the blue tits, who immediately stop their feeding to sit watching and scolding their bigger relative. They don't approach the larger bird, and the great tit, for its part, seems completely unbothered by their intolerance of it. The interloper sits there for a few moments before it flies off again, and as soon as it has gone one of the blue tits is straight down to the box, landing on the roof, examining it minutely before acrobatically hopping to the entrance hole and peering in. The blue tits are evidently worried they will get gazumped in the highly competitive housing market.

The other boxes in the garden have elicited no known interest as of yet. I have another hole-nesting box just like the one the blue tits are building in, but the diameter of the hole is bigger and could suit the great tit that has just caused the blue tits so much consternation. Great tits nested in it two years ago, so it will obviously be suitable for them if they choose to use it. I also have an open-fronted robin box tucked into the ivy-clad wall. Last year a pair of robins used it to rear three chicks, much to our delight, so fingers are crossed that it will be used as before. A pair of robins have certainly been regulars in the lower garden since mid-February, singing for us in return for their mealworms; they are obviously holding territory around the garden and its environs, and they are supremely confident around us. It looks promising, but then there are a myriad of other natural sites they could choose if they wished; still, if you build it they will come. Probably.

Spring walks

The woodland I am walking through is alive with life. There is a rude abundance to it; the leaves are out, the various shades of fresh green break up the skeletal dendrite shapes once more, and bird song is everywhere: a repetitive song thrush sings from high up, a willow warbler from low down, their melodies jarred by a chiffchaff, and then the metallic call of a great spotted woodpecker. I pause in my progress and lean my back against the large stem of a pedunculate oak as it towers upwards, away from the woodland floor, I stand there, supported by decades of timber growth, and observe the woodland around me, watching the to and fro of birds and insects, listening to their song and the buzzing drone. The carpet of bluebells fans out in front of me, glossy green and beautiful blue, abruptly stopping to be replaced by the duller, more uniform green of dog's mercury to my right, where the composition of the soil obviously but invisibly changes. Then, looking further right I can see where the green of the dog's mercury is interrupted by the brown of soil pushed up into mounds. A badger sett. Well-walked pathways through the sea of green emanate out from these tumps, a spider-web of trails through the wood.

A movement catches my eye back around to my left. I turn slowly from the direction of the sett to find the cause: a roe doe, delicately, carefully, warily stepping through the wood. She stops a moment, a black nose twitches, testing the air for scent, two ears turn, listening for danger. But her keen senses detect nothing alarming, so she lowers her head and browses at the ash saplings that have been struggling in the low light of the woodland floor, their struggle for light now ended by the feeding of this graceful herbivore.

She is pregnant, her load visible to me even at this distance; the twins[17] she is carrying will be born very soon, perhaps even within the next couple of days. She pauses in her browsing, lifts her head and neck up, scans about with her eyes and twists her large ears this way and that before returning to feed once more. She does this at regular intervals, conscious that when her head is down low to the ground her early warning detection

---

17 Roe generally give birth to twins, although occasionally they may have just one kid.

system is compromised. She raises her head again, this time with more alacrity. Her parabolic-like ears turn to the side, her face and eyes follow; she has heard something and doesn't like it. She stands stock still, save for the slow, deliberate chewing movement of her lower jaw. Then I hear it, faintly, carried on the breath of air that is passing through the trees: children's voices. They seem a long way off, but she is evidently unnerved by what she hears. Experience will have taught her that human noises can sometimes mean dogs, and she can't afford to be chased, not now, not when she is so heavily pregnant.

For several more seconds she stands still, her head, with its array of detection systems, the nose, the ears and the eyes, all pointing towards where the sound is emanating from. Then, slowly, she lowers her head back down to the woodland floor, moving a step forward as she does so before continuing to browse the vegetation once again. I can no longer hear the sound, but then I could barely hear it in the first place. The doe has evidently satisfied herself that its cause is moving away from her. Gradually she moves about the woodland in front of me, changing her position as she does so until she is facing directly away from me, her heart-shaped rump patch[18] pointed towards where I am standing – a rump patch that can flash white when danger is sensed, but is currently subdued as she feeds. This angle reveals her pregnancy to me more than ever, the large bulge in her body looking incongruous when compared to her lean, delicate legs.

Roe are highly unusual in the deer world. They follow a breeding strategy shared with the badgers which slumber beneath the woodland floor that we are standing on. The roe rut is in late July and August; she would have mated with a buck then, and her eggs would have been fertilised, but they wouldn't have started to develop. Instead, in a process known as delayed implantation, the eggs would have stayed dormant until the new year dawned – and then, and only then, they would have implanted themselves in the wall of her uterus and started their development. No other deer exhibit this breeding strategy; in fact no other hoofed animal does.[19]

My limbs are beginning to ache; the long period of inactivity is beginning to take its toll. I haven't moved a muscle since I first saw the doe picking her way through the vegetation, and the bark of the oak tree, supportive at first, is now feeling like the gnarled uneven surface that it is. Uncomfortable pressures from its unyielding ridges are making my stay uncomfortable, but I can't make her run; to do so would be as unfair as it would be reckless. I continue watching her, experiencing the quandary of pleasure in being able to watch this wild mammal whilst wishing she would move on. Eventually she does so, carefully, gracefully, picking her way through the vegetation, losing herself in the abundant woodland flora, finally allowing me to move, to stretch my aching muscles, muscles that remind me of their discomfort every step of the way home.

---

18 The rump patch of the roe is a good way to distinguish between male and female: where the doe has a heart-shaped patch, the buck has a kidney-shaped one.

19 Information on the breeding of roe deer taken from the Mammal Society website: www.mammal.org.uk .

The morning dawns with a slight chill, but the warmth of the sun is already banishing the nip in the air as we leave the house and walk up through the village. We turn down one of the lanes, dropping down to where it crosses the stream before climbing steeply up the rolling countryside of mid-Devon. A Raven cronks above us, a joyous sound and one that makes us stop our walk to find this large corvid, the largest passerine, as it flies somewhere above us. It is not hard to spot; a buzzard-sized bird, jet-black with long wings and wedge-shaped tail showing clearly against the deep blue of the sky. A second bird is flying to join it. Both birds have a relaxed manner to them, and the distinctive calling of the two birds can only be described as a happy sound; the first enforces this interpretation by folding its wings and tumbling sideways, falling through the sky before opening its wings and continuing onwards, calling once again.

Ravens are birds that wear their emotions for all to see and hear. Their evocative call conveys many emotions – there are happy cronks and unhappy cronks, and a whole gamut of others in between. If you spend much time with these birds you begin to be able to understand the meaning of these calls; you can tell when they are unhappy just by listening, just as I could tell these two birds were happy from hearing them call. The tumbling somersaults that ravens perform are another sign of their mood; no one quite knows why they do it, but they certainly enjoy it – it is a move full of exuberance, it looks like fun. The happy, tumbling ravens continue on their flight, diverging from us as we continue our linear walk along the lane, discussing their happy acrobatics as we go.

The high earth banks on either side of us begin to reduce in height, allowing the light to reach in and warm the bank sides. Where the sun reaches it is celebrated by the delicate white flowers of the greater stitchwort, sprinkles of white across a bank of green. Small birds are dashing about these hedge banks; some will still be building their nests, others working hard to feed the chicks within their already finished structures. There is a busyness in the air. We take the more relaxed approach, stopping at a conveniently placed bench at a lane junction and settling down to watch the hustle and bustle about us.

Behind the bench, but concealed by the remnants of an old boundary fence, there lies a pond, and from somewhere within it a moorhen startles us with its loud explosive call. On the lane a male pied wagtail, looking very dapper in his smart black and white livery, walks along the tarmac, suddenly rushing forward after an insect before stopping and pumping his tail vigorously. Away over the fields a buzzard is circling, angling its wings to catch the thermal and gain height without expending effort; two rooks take affront at the raptor's presence and noisily make their way towards the bigger bird, laboriously flapping their black wings as they close in on it. The buzzard responds by increasing the angle of its wings and tightening the soaring circles it has been tracing in the sky. It gains height rapidly, leaving the would-be mobbers to shout their displeasure from below before they give up on their futile effort and return in the direction they had come.

Onwards we walk, choosing a leisurely pace more akin to the buzzard than the energy-expending rooks that tried to mob it, walking past rambling brambles and

The mazy ramblings of leaf miners are natural works of art that decorate many a bramble leaf.

reading the scrawled graffiti of the leaf miners on last year's growth, whilst new shoots begin their rampage forth. The micro-millimetre world of the bramble leaf miner is a mazy meander between the upper and lower outer surfaces of the wafer-thin leaves. Tracing these silvery reminders of last year's peregrinations shows you their progress, detailing their growth within the confines of the leaf as their minings get broader, their twists and turns at times interrupted by the harder, tougher seams of the leaf's veins, canalising their silver route until it can either break through the barrier or turn off into yet more labyrinthine ramblings. These bramble leafminers are the larval stages of micro moths,[20] exploiting a habitat and a food resource that is almost another dimension away from our own three-dimensional world.

The lane we are following mimics the seemingly random turns of the leaf miners, twisting and turning for no apparent reason as only the best Devon lanes do. As we come around a long, sweeping left bend we see the large barn on our right and immediately drop our voices. One end of the open-sided barn has a stack of precariously piled hay bales; the far end, though, is clear, and up in the beams and rafters of this end is a large wooden

20 The commonest of these is *Stigmella aurella*.

box that looks like a strange type of elevated chicken coop. It has been deliberately placed there, and it is in use. It is the reason our own ramblings have drawn us here: through the angled stems of an old coppiced hazel we can see the box's occupier perched atop it, a white smudge in an otherwise timber-coloured subfusc environment: an adult barn owl, its head slightly lowered and its eyes closed as it sleeps in the afternoon, resting before its day ahead – a day that will only start as our own ends.

We sometimes catch glimpses of these white apparitions as they ghost over the road at the entrance to the village on their night-time hunting missions, targeting the voles and mice of the rough broad road verge. To see one like this, completely at ease, is a real treat. A barn owl in its eponymous barn. Barn owls are one of the few British birds that have, like the house martin and the house sparrow, a man-made feature as part of their name because of their close nesting association with our own structures. Open barns were once much more common in the landscape than they are now, but the rush to convert these structures into money-making properties has had a big impact on the white owl, reducing the availability of breeding sites for these truly beautiful birds. It is great to see that the owner of this barn has not only kept it open and usable, but has also provided the birds with a readymade starter home, a conservation conversion if you like.

We walk on along the lane, careful not to disturb the sleeping owl, looking back once through the hedge to see the almost glowing white shape in the shadows of the barn as it snoozes on its box, a box that symbolises all that can be right between us and the wildlife we share our spaces with. It shows that there is room for us and wildlife in our highly managed landscapes.

I am very much an advocate of rewilding, of allowing nature to manage its spaces, but in a crowded island like ours the majority, the vast majority, of land is dominated by us humans and our 'management' of it. Such a resource-hungry species as ours will always have an impact on wildlife, but we can mitigate it, we can allow nature to be part of all our lives. It is a repeat of the childhood lesson that our parents would try to impart; we need to learn to share. Our relationship with nature is an odd one; we may forget that we are part of nature, just a mammal that evolved in Africa, we may get troubled by the fact that the rest of nature will happily go on without us. But we can coexist with wildlife in our everyday lives; all we have to do, just as the owner of the barn has done, is allow it to happen.

The laughing call of a green woodpecker rings out across the moor. I look down towards the sound, to catch sight of the bird undulating its way back to the large beech trees that act as a windbreak to the scattering of houses beyond, the brightness of the woodpecker's rump delineating its bouncing flight as it heads back to the comfort of the trees. Woodpeckers aren't birds of the open moor, but the green does use the interface between the small village and the moorland that surrounds it. The beech trees planted many years ago to deflect the worst of the south-westerlies have matured, their crowns wind-blown and gloriously scruffy; there is dead wood in the trees, torn limbs to provide cavities for the birds to nest in. Beyond those trees are grassy paddocks and more arboreal delineations. Many of the buds on the beech have burst open, the leaves now unfurling, bright green delights decorating the landscape.

On the moorland side of these towering windbreaks the vegetation is very short. The wandering livestock of the open ground know that this area provides some shelter from the bad weather so they often concentrate here, and the concentration of grazing pressure and accumulated enrichment from their dung has changed the vegetation from a mosaic of heather, gorse and grasses into a short-turfed, scruffy lawn. It was this lawn that the green woodpecker flew up from, the short grass providing the perfect habitat for its favourite food, ants.

A flash of white from the edge of this moorland lawn reveals another maintainer of its turf; the white is the scuttling scut of a rabbit as it heads back to the cover of an unruly gorse bush that has collapsed in on itself, creating a fortified spiny shelter for it to take sanctuary within. The green woodpecker laughs again and flies along the line of beeches, landing on the smooth grey trunk of one, momentarily in view before it scrambles around the trunk and out of sight.

I turn back around and follow the stoned track out onto the moor. As I rise I pass more and more lumps of scattered granite and see another flash of white – but this time it is avian in origin, not mammalian. The white rump of a male wheatear signals my presence to his as yet unseen mate as he flies away from me; he perches up on a convenient lump of hard granite and clicks his disapproval of my presence. Censured by the censored. 'Wheatear' is not this bird's name; not its original one in any case, as the name was given to the bird to protect sensitive ears from its true name, 'white arse'.

The white arse was the name given to these spring and summer visitors, but its name was considered far too vulgar for polite society, so when the early naturalists, the educated and refined persons that they were, began to write about our wildlife they deliberately censored the name, opting to call it something that was more acceptable to their tastes. The problem was they couldn't call it 'white ear' as the bird doesn't have that feature, so instead they opted for the name it now holds, a name that paints an inaccurate picture of the bird's habits. These birds don't feed on wheat – they are invertebrate eaters – nor do they inhabit wheat fields, preferring open, stony habitat, like the moor I am on now. The writers even put into print deliberate lies about the bird's behaviour, stating that the birds get fat from the spilled seeds of the ears of wheat to be found in the fields. Oh, the webs we weave.[21]

I walk past the unknowing victim of prudish censorship, leaving him to scold others who dare to walk in his territory. The path takes me higher before dropping down towards a steep wooded valley. As I descend, the vegetation begins to change; the patches of gorse increase in size, and in between them bracken is already springing forth. The

---

21 'Flash of Colour': article on the wheatear by Ian Parsons in *Bird Watching*, March 2019.

The male wheatear is a striking bird; but in case you miss it, it flashes yet more white at you as it flies away.

tightly curled knobs of early spring are now unfurling tentacles, racing upwards with one another, preparing to close their canopy over the remnants of last year's stems. Then the trees begin. Scrubby hawthorns and scruffy downy birches gradually give way to sessile oak, which soon dominates the valley sides. Within a few minutes of entering the woodland, I hear the first spinning-coin-like song of a wood warbler, a series of sharp metallic notes, increasing in speed before merging into one another in an aural blur. It takes me a while to spot one; they are leaf warblers, like the chiffchaff, and spend their time up in the canopy of the trees, in amongst the fresh leaves, and always – it seems to me at least – with the sun behind them.

Eventually I home in on the distinctive song and see one high up, the bright white underside and lemon-yellow face and throat giving the bird a fresh appearance on this equally fresh spring day. It is a welcome sight, to go with the welcome sound of its song. Wood warblers are not common birds, restricted mainly, as they are, to the western upland oak woodlands of the country; there are only around 6,500 breeding pairs in Britain[22] and their numbers are declining. These attractive little warblers are struggling to fit into our modern world. The bird above me, busy establishing his territory after a migration flight from sub-Saharan Africa, once more sings his rapid tumbling song, a spinning £2 coin on a worktop, a coin that weighs the same as the singer above me.

As I pick my way down through the trees I spot another spring migrant, this one lower down, darting out from a disorderly-looking holly, a black and white bird on a sortie, living up to its name as it plucks a fly out of the woodland air before returning to its perch in the prickly understory. A male pied flycatcher is a captivating beauty of a bird that is exactly what its name suggests. Out it dashes once more, this time hanging momentarily, wings and tail feathers spread, as it snaps its bill around another small

---

22 Woodward et al, *British Birds*, vol.113.

flying insect. It is a privilege to be able to watch these two specialised insect-eating migrants, each one filling a slightly different niche. I watch the two-tone flycatcher for several minutes before leaving him to his flycatching, I carry on, picking my way down the slope, through the increasing understory of holly and hazel, until I come out on the path that runs along the turbulent river at the valley bottom.

I perch myself on a moss-clad rock and watch the celerity of the water as it smashes itself recklessly against the numerous rocks and broken trunks that line the river's course. The water's noise blends in with the song of many birds: the wood warbler still spins its song, a song thrush reiterates its every note, and a chaffinch tumbles to its flourishing finish before starting all over again. The song and the water empty my mind of its clutter, and I just sit there for several minutes, lost in the riparian woodland. Eventually the cold dampness of the moss persuades me to rise back up again, to enter the human world once more and continue my walk. I follow the muddy-puddle path for several hundred yards before striking off up through the woodland, angling across the contours, climbing steadily, feeling the steepness of the slope tugging at my legs.

On the edge of the woodland, a once-giant beech, probably planted as a boundary marker many years ago, has been thoroughly deracinated by the wind that races across the open moor beyond. The remains of the giant overlapping brackets of the appropriately named giant polypore fungus protrude outwards from the fluted base of the now-horizontal trunk. The fungus would have attacked the tree's roots, making them brittle and vulnerable to failure; even in sheltered locations a beech tree attacked by this fungus would have become unstable, and here, where woodland meets moor, the tree stood no chance. The once-immaculate, sinuous smooth grey bark of its trunk is already degrading, and the cracks are showing as the protective skin of the tree within begins to fall apart. The once expansive, arm-like main branches that had leant out towards the open space, chasing and dominating the sunlight, now lie in shattered pieces, broken by the impact of the old tree smashing into the unyielding surface of the moor.

The tree has been down for some time and due to the inaccessible terrain it has avoided the usual fate of such a windfall. The effort required to convert this once-majestic tree into firewood, not to mention the effort needed to transport the logs down off the moor afterwards, has obviously proved unattractive to the locals. Although humans might not want it, nature does: it is rapidly reclaiming it, recycling the tree's ingredients for others to use. There is always something shocking about seeing a large tree ripped from the ground, torn from its medium. To us, these trees can seem immortal, their relatively long lives far beyond us in both physical reality and imagination. The sight of a majestic tree lying spavined on the earth instead of towering upwards towards the sky, is an unpleasant reminder of our own mortality. But the tree's tenuous grip on life is, like our own, easily released.

Lost in these profound thoughts, I leave the toppled arboreal leviathan behind me. As I head out over the open moor, back into the realm of the white-arsed wheatears, it is not long before I am scolded again for my impudence.

From the darkness

Many trees have a characteristic shape to them, rendering them identifiable from a distance in the landscape. But the yew tree is not one of those; it follows no rules. It is found in a myriad of forms: single-stemmed, multi-stemmed, flat crown, round crown, spiky crown, tall, squat, spreading, compact … when it comes to form the anarchic yew doesn't follow any convention. Yet it is identifiable at a distance; there is one feature that connects all yews, no matter what shape they pursue, and that is darkness. Yew trees have a brooding air to them, a presence. They are a dark tree, but in that darkness there is beauty.

We've paused on a walk around the lanes at the local churchyard, a place where two large, clean-stemmed and spiky -crowned yews exert their dominance over the graves of generations of humans laid out beneath them. Nearby are the tidier cultivated 'Irish' yews planted in a neat row, but these are dwarfed and made irrelevant by their wilder, unruly originators. These two arboreal giants not only pre-date the humans buried amongst their roots; they could even pre-date the church itself. The area in which the church now stands has long been of supernatural significance. The religion may have changed, but the site hasn't.

Nearby there is a woodhenge dating from 3,000 BCE, and numerous locations in the vicinity have old names linking them to a druid-dominated past where the woods were

Churchyards are great places to find wonderful examples of the unruly yew.

sacred and the Green Man dwelt. The River Yeo, which flows through this landscape, has even been described as Devon's Ganges, such was its past significance.[23] Yews have long played a part in our religious superstitions as important symbols that were purposefully incorporated into the new churchyards of the new religion.

Close up to the tree that Shakespeare described as the 'double-fatal yew',[24] you can feel its imposing presence. The Bard's phrase refers to the tree's use in the manufacture of deadly weapons – the lethal longbows of Agincourt – as well as its deadly toxicity. Nearly all the parts of the tree are poisonous: its timber, bark, needles and seeds; even the sawdust and the pollen are considered a health hazard. But one part isn't, and that is the drop of red that is the aril surrounding the tree's precious seed. Often wrongly referred to as yew berries, these are actually highly modified cones, for the yew is a conifer, one of only three conifers native to the UK.[25]

The red aril is sweet in taste for those willing to risk trying it, but the seed contained within is the tree's most deadly part, so trying it would be a risk indeed, and one that cannot be recommended. The sweetness of the aril is an enticement, a payment for the safe delivery of the seed. It is the thrushes who are the main couriers, the blackbird and mistle joined by wintering redwing and fieldfare. The tree rewards them not just with the sticky flesh of the aril but by also spreading the ripening of them over a period of three months, providing a sustained source of food during the winter months.

The seeds pass through the simplistic avian gut unharmed, deposited elsewhere in the droppings of the birds to maybe germinate and grow themselves. But mammalian guts are too thorough in their processing, the digestive juices breaking down the seed's hard casing, rendering it unviable and releasing the poison at the same time. In human terms, the yew doesn't want its seed wasted and makes sure it punishes those that attempt to do so.

While we stand in the churchyard admiring the two dark trees a male chaffinch, his plumage a vivid brightness amongst the darkness of green, studiously picks his way along one of the sprawling branches, checking the dishevelled bark for food before flying to the top of the neighbouring mass of dark green foliage from where he briefly sings his tumble of notes – and then he is gone, leaving the trees to brood in silence.

But it is only a localised silence; beyond the churchyard a clump of common lime trees tower up above all others, and from their lofty tops comes the raucous din of a rookery. Partially concealed behind the heart-shaped leaves of lime green, the scruffy stick nests of the rooks' breeding colony are a hive of activity. Each nest now has three or even four black-feathered chicks crammed within, each one craving to be fed by returning parents. Adults call to the young, the young call to the adults, and the nesting neighbours bicker with one another in a constant cacophonous chorus of harsh corvid shouts. It is a brilliant noise.

---

23 *Wildwood, A Journey Through Trees*, Roger Deakin, Penguin, 2008. One of the best books I have ever read!
24 A quote from William Shakespeare's *Richard II*.
25 The other two being Scots Pine and Common Juniper.

We leave behind us the quietness of the dark yews and the din of the rabble of dark rooks as we follow the lane back towards the village, walking and talking. Lost in our world, we could have so easily missed what happened next. But we didn't. A brown length dashed across the lane, from one bank to the next, chased by its own black-tipped tail. A moment of pure mustelid magic. A stoat, the black tip to the tail diagnostic, giving us the briefest of views as it bounded over the tarmac surface of the lane. A mini-carnivore living its life at a very different speed from ours. The blur of the stoat was gone in a second, but the memory of it is timeless.

Mouse-shaped spears, mustelids,[26] have always fascinated me. From an early obsession with badgers to keeping a house-trained ferret that had free rein of our home, these predacious mammals have long captured my imagination. Britain is a country shorn of its large predators, extirpated long ago, but our miniature ones – the stoat and the weasel – still reign over their respective realms despite the continued battle waged against them by those that value game interests over our native wildlife.

The weasel is the smallest carnivore in the world, measuring no more in length than the breadth of the stretched-out fingers on my hand, using its small size to hunt down mice and voles within their own tunnels. The stoat is a bit bigger, up to about a foot in length[27] and whilst small mammals feature in its diet the stoat is rightly famed as a rabbit-killer, tackling these much bigger and heavier mammals with ease. Neither stoats nor weasels are known for giving us long views, and the view we just had of the stoat is typical, a glimpse of it as it hurtles through our world. But every mustelid sighting is a special one.

Another mustelid is also living in these parts, although so far we have only see them dead, cut down on the roads around the village. But as oxymoronic as it seems, these road kills are a positive sign, indicative of the return of the species from its human-induced nadir. Polecats were once widespread across Britain but, being bigger than the closely related stoat and weasel, they were considered as a pest, as vermin, as something to be killed for the greater good.

And they were indeed killed, in vast numbers, very nearly becoming extinct so that one hundred years ago they were confined to just a few areas in Wales. The hostility shown to the polecat in the countryside only lessened when we humans turned our hostility on each other. It was between the two world wars that the intensity of persecution against the polecat significantly declined, easing the pressure on these beautiful animals and allowing them to slowly recover their numbers. The First World War removed many men from the countryside, especially those such as gamekeepers, with firearms experience; many never came back, and the end of the war also saw the beginning of the end of many large game-rearing estates, estates that in the brutality and darkness of the human conflict had lost not only their employees but also their heirs.

The polecats have now spread outwards from the principality, reaching as far east as the Brecklands of East Anglia. They have travelled north, with animals now recorded

---

26 From the Latin *mus* for mouse and *telum* for spear, missile, weapon.

27 Measurements adapted from the Mammal Society website: www.mammal.org.uk.

regularly in Cumbria, and south to the Channel; they have even made it back to where I live, in the heart of Devon – a welcome return, and an example of how tenacious nature can be if we stop killing it. To me, the warm reddish-brown blur of a stoat was a very welcome sight; perhaps soon it will be that much darker mustelid that we see crossing our path.

The beauty in scruffiness

Cow parsley lines the road, swaying to and fro in the wake of passing traffic, abuzz with insects, umbelliferous lines of creamy white. An abundance of hoverflies hang in the air above them, a variety of colours and patterns, their flight skills a joy to behold, unshackled movement in all directions: forwards, backwards, up, down and everything in between. There is a late sunny afternoon feel to the late sunny afternoon; spring has almost completely sprung, and everywhere is abundant growth and busy activity.

I clamber over the mossy stile and onto the soft grass of the footpath as it meanders along the sinuous curves of the river. The water flows lazily through the alder-thrown dappled shade, and a small bird flies upstream, flashing bright yellow as it zips through a window of sunlight, the light reflecting the glory of its plumage. Someone once said

The glorious grey wagtail is a bird that definitely deserves a better name.

that a named thing is a tamed thing,[28] and it is very true that the name of this bird does indeed tame its beauty. 'Grey wagtail' is a name which to the uninitiated conjures up something drab and dull; it certainly doesn't paint a picture of vibrant yellow contrasting with a black bib and pure white stripes on the bird's face – but that is what a grey wagtail has.

Grey wagtails are glorious birds. The male in particular, in his breeding finery, is one of the most exotic-looking members of the British avifauna, while the female, with her more subdued plumage, has a more delicate yellow hue; but she is no grey bird, not by any stretch. The grey wagtail does have a grey back and crown, but to name it after that rather than its other colours is unfair. The problem lies with its relatives: the yellow wagtail, a summer migrant to our shores, and the citrine wagtail, a rare vagrant from the East, are close relatives of the misnamed grey. All three look superficially similar, and all three have large splashes of yellow in their plumage, but it appears that the first two used up all the available yellow when it came to naming this tail-wagging trio.

Blissfully ignorant of its human label and with its tail pumping furiously, the male wagtail hops from exposed stone to exposed stone as the water flows past. Suddenly it jumps upwards – a vertical dash at some flies overhead – and again the brilliant yellow catches the sunlight, a dazzling flash from within the penumbra cast by the branches overhead, then back down to the stone, tail working furiously at the rear. I see the broken fly slotted neatly in its dark slender beak; this is a bird that has young to feed. It is soon off the rock and flying downstream, back towards where the river narrows and squeezes under the old stone bridge that carries the lane across it. Somewhere in that old stonework will be a hole or a ledge that has a collection of poorly named young waiting for a meal.

I walk on, watching the blue tits hanging like acrobats off the tips of the twigs of the alders. As they check the tree's small wooden cones for any hiding invertebrate a group of tinkling goldfinches flies overhead, their golden wing bars flashing in competition with the grey wagtail earlier. The river bends away from the course of the path that I am following, taking me up the hill, through the long ungrazed grass. A kestrel is hanging high above the slope, tail fanned out, wings beating steady time to maintain its position in the airflow, keeping its head stock still. The steadied head, elevated above the field, can examine all below it in blurless clarity. A careless movement is all it is looking for, but no movement comes and it stops beating its wings and folds the tail in, dropping a few feet, before flying onwards on steady clipped wing beats to try its luck elsewhere.

I leave the field and head into a tangled slice of woodland that has sprung up around what would have been old small-scale quarry workings. As I enter the shady interior a wood pigeon clatters into flight above me and the sharp tang of fox enters my nostrils. Ivy is everywhere, covering the ground as much as it covers the motley collection of stems and trunks. Here and there a tree has toppled, losing its grip on the stony ground, pitching over into one of its neighbours, forming a jumble of angled wood. To progress

28 Joanne Harris, author of many books including the best-selling *Chocolat*.

Scruffy, forgotten corners of the countryside like this one are important places for many species.

through it I have to lean and duck and clamber; there are no straight lines to follow here. A nuthatch is working its way down one of the vertical trunks, probing the bark with its bill, its headlong progress stopped by the climbing ivy. Thwarted, it flies across to another, barer, trunk, landing high up before walking down the vertical stem as if gravity were nothing more than a passing irritation to it. The bandit-faced bird disappears around the reverse of the trunk to continue its probing unobserved.

A great spotted woodpecker announces itself with its loud call as it flies in through the leafy canopy, but I lose sight of it in the tangle of stems and branches above me. There is plenty of evidence on the older stems of woodpeckers using this ragged sliver of woodland, a long-dead and now rapidly degrading pine stem has four old oval holes carved into it, old nest holes from years gone by. There will be another hole nearby, in a tree not nearly so dilapidated, and within that hole young woodpeckers will be listening eagerly for evidence that the next meal is about to be delivered. A small coal tit flies among the branches, eyeing every bit of them for food, then a wren pops out from the ivy carpet, flies up to a branch, cocks its little tail skywards and shouts out its song. From higher up a chaffinch chinks and a mistle thrush rattles out its call, whilst all around the ivy twitches this way and that as a result of unseen scurrying. The place is alive with life.

These tatty, scruffy corners of our countryside are some of the best habitats we have for wildlife, yet they are often viewed as needing something, needing our management and our guidance. The truth is they don't. These wild little corners just need to be left to their own devices, as free as possible from our influence. They are vital oases in our overmanaged land, and we need more of them. They don't have to be large; they just need to be fenced off and forgotten, left for nature to rule over once again. Little realms of scruffiness in our all-too-tidy world.

Dimpsy doings

The air is heavy and clingy. The warm humidity of the day has continued, even though the daylight is now following the sun westwards. The blackbirds in the forest around me start to get nervous as the light rapidly melts away, panicked calls ringing out from them in the dimpsy air.

The word 'dimpsy' is quite probably a new one for you, but to me it is a perfectly normal word that just as perfectly sums up the quality of the light as the day slips into the night. The English dictionary defines the word as 'dusk, twilight' before stating that it is Devonshire in origin.[29] Until I lived elsewhere I never knew it was peculiar to where I grew up; strange looks would follow if I ever happened to say it in conversation, but it is a great little word. It is the light that is now enveloping me as I wait patiently on the track by the young pine plantation.

The stems of the mature pines further off begin to slowly dissolve into one another. The light thickens, shadows merge and become the background themselves – and then, just as your eyes are telling you that it is getting too dark, just as the blackbirds finally give up on their panic, a nightjar begins its wonderful song. I find it impossible to describe this amazing sound. There are no onomatopoeic words that can capture its essence. Some people describe it as a mechanical sound, an outboard motor or a sewing machine, but that is so wrong; there is nothing mechanical about it, it is not manufactured, and we shouldn't fall into the age-old trap of comparing everything we see or hear to our own species and our dubious achievements. The song of the nightjar is just that: an enigmatic song from an enigmatic bird. It is a beautiful and evocative sound. It is the song of dimpsy light.

A column of gnats dance their vertical ballet in front of me, as other related flies concentrate their attention on the exposed skin of my head. It is an unwritten rule that if you're getting bitten by midges, it's a good night for nightjars. As I console myself with that thought, a second bird starts up, closer to me than the first, and the two songs meet in the air and merge into one another, creating an almost disorientating sound that seems to wrap itself about me. I am lost within the song. It's impossible for me to distinguish the two separate singers until the first suddenly, abruptly, winds down and the flow of notes audibly slows; and then, as if in appreciation of its efforts, there is a clap.

29 *Oxford English Dictionary*, Oxford University Press, 1993.

But this is no self-congratulatory round of applause; it is the solitary clap made by the bird's wings as it takes to the air.[30]

I soon see it, silhouetted against the sky, as it glides hawk like over the young trees beneath it, ghosting through the sky in complete silence before once more making that clapping sound with its wings, a territorial noise that gets a response from the other, still singing, bird, whose volume seems to ratchet up another notch. The sky still has a red tinge to it as the nightjar bisects it, the specialised fringed feathers of the bird's wings damping any sound from them. These are birds that fly in stealth mode – but at the moment it is not hunting: it is, to use colloquial parlance, showing off.

Seemingly pleased with its efforts the bird suddenly twists downwards, as it does so it flashes the white wing and tail patches that mark it as a male. The patches seem to glow in the near-darkness as the bird pitches on to an old upturned root plate, folding its wings and tail and abruptly turning off the white as it lands on a crooked, finger-like lateral root that points forlornly in the direction of the remaining red glow. It lands along the root, not across it, for nightjars have small, weak feet that are incapable of perching across a branch in the more typical pose of other bird species. The tiny bill opens, revealing the huge gape of the bird, and it unleashes its song once more, turning its head from side to side as it does so, broadcasting its unique song to all corners of the young plantation. Another nightjar silhouettes across the sky, a slow glide before a rapid burst on those muffled wings as it charges upwards and plucks an insect out of the air before dropping lower, vanishing in the blackness of the background of mature forest. These late migrants have only been with us for a couple of weeks; I haven't seen them since last July, when I went out deliberately to find them. It has been a long wait to see, and hear, these magnificent crepuscular[31] birds once again. My nightjar thirst slaked, I steal off into the night, using the moonlight to navigate my way along the forest track, crunching the loose stones as I walk, and listening to the seemingly unending song of the nightjars as the sound follows me through the darkness.

The European nightjar is the only member of its family to breed in Britain. Its name is a derivative of 'nightchurr', another attempt to put into words the bird's unique song. This is a bird that has had many names, including nighthawk in reference to its raptorial silhouette, and fern owl, a name that comes from its nocturnal habits and silent flight as well as a preference for habitats that often include bracken.

My favourite alternative name, though, is goatsucker, a name built entirely on misunderstanding, but one that sticks fast in the mind. Nightjars are often found on heathy ground, uncultivated land that hasn't been improved by agriculture, the sort of land which was often common land and used by people to graze their small flocks of livestock on. Goats would often be grazed on such land, browsing its coarser vegetation

---

30 A recent paper has strongly challenged the idea that the clap sound is made by the wings coming together; it suggests that instead the clap is probably generated by the physical structures of the feathers themselves, making a whiplash-style crack in the air: 'A review of "wing-clapping" in European Nightjars', Mark J Eddowes and Alison J Lea, *British Birds* Vol 114, No 10, October 2021.

31 Active at dawn and dusk – or, if you prefer, when 'tis dimpsy.

with ease, Nightjars feed over these habitats, and as they take insects from out of the air are unworried by any livestock on them; it may even be that they are attracted to feed close to the livestock, as the animals will attract insects as well as disturbing others into flight as they browse.

For a shepherd steeped in folk tales, seeing this strange dark shadow of a bird flitting close to his charges, watching it swoop downwards, disappearing around the livestock as it blended into the shadows before suddenly reappearing again elsewhere as it emerged above the horizon, it would have been easy to think that something odd was going on. From somewhere now lost in the dimpsy light of the past, the belief that these strange birds drank the milk of the goats as they grazed the commons was born.[32]

Nightjars are of course insectivorous, catching their prey on the wing, hunting down moths and snaffling flying beetles and bugs as well as a wide variety of flies, including the ones that feed on you as you watch the birds feeding on them. During the day they use their exquisitely marked plumage to stay undetected on the ground, blending into their surroundings, transforming from the graceful black silhouettes of the late evening into unseen mysteries of the bare ground. These are birds that take their camouflage seriously. The soft plumage, a subtle, mottled mix of browns, buff white and greys, is an obvious visual camouflage, but these same feathers also camouflage the bird in flight. The silent flight of the nightjar is no evolutionary accident; it is there to allow the bird to silently approach moths – moths which are able to hear predatory noises such as wing flaps and take avoiding action. But they don't hear the coming of the nightjar.

The plumage renders them hard to detect on the ground during daylight, but predators are canny foes, so the nightjar takes it further still. Like most species that are active in low light conditions, the nightjar has relatively large eyes. These big eyes may not be obvious to our own tamed and curbed food-finding instincts, but they are definitely detectable to a hungry hunter. If a nightjar hears or sees potential danger approaching it will carefully watch it – but not with wide-open eyes; it watches with squinted eyes, the camouflaged lids held almost shut, just open enough to allow the bird to observe what is happening around it, but not open enough to reveal the large round shape of the eye.[33]

But the visual trickery doesn't stop there. Nightjars don't make a nest, there is no construction of twigs or grasses; instead they opt to lay their two eggs on bare ground and incubate them by simply sitting over the top of them. But nesting on bare ground in open habitats means that the bird will spend at least part of the day in sunshine, and sunshine produces shadows. A bird-shaped shadow is bound to attract attention, so the nightjar negates this risk by sitting in an elongated and compact way, facing the sun, edging around with it during the day, preventing its own shadow from reaching the ground by its perfect posture and positioning. Nightjars just don't want to be seen.

Nor do they want to be smelt. Many predators hunt by scent; watch a fox hunting and you will see that it is constantly using its nose, sniffing the ground and the air, trying

32 The scientific name *Caprimulgus europaeus* means European Goatsucker.

33 A related species in South America takes this further: the common potoo has notches in its eyelids enabling it to see even when its eyes are shut.

to discern a scent that may lead it to its next meal. Because our human nose is so poor at detecting scent, this is a world that we little understand, but there is certainly a lot of anecdotal evidence to suggest that nightjars are able to either suppress their scent or change it so that it doesn't attract attention when they are nesting. I can remember many years ago when I was watching an area where I knew there to be a female nightjar sitting on eggs, and to my horror a pair of cocker spaniels, released with ignorant abandon by their owner, ran all over the site, nose to ground, investigating everything. I watched them find the small scuff mark I had made in the soil a few metres from the nest to act as a marker to me if I needed to relocate the nest for ringing. The dogs explored this thoroughly with their noses, moving around the immediate area, including where the bird was nesting. I expected her to fly at any minute, abandoning her eggs or chicks to escape herself. But no bird flew.

When the dogs had moved on, no doubt to rampage over other areas where ground-nesting birds cowered whilst their owner blithely walked on by, I headed to the site, expecting to find an abandoned nest site. Something had obviously happened to the nest and it had failed; why else hadn't the bird flown? But I was wrong to think that, because just a couple of metres from my mark the female nightjar was sitting tight on the ground, still on her nest, watching me from behind her almost-closed eyelids. Her camouflage had not just defeated the spaniels' eyesight, but had also beaten their famous nose.

Distractions

Beautiful late spring sunshine bathes the garden in its warmth; everywhere is abuzz with insects and all manner of bees are visiting the flowers, but one species is also visiting my home-made bee hotel that I carefully placed so that it gets the maximum amount of sunlight available. I made my hotel out of an old square oak gatepost that I had salvaged. Its base was completely rotten, the post long toppled, but the top section of it was still sound and perfect for me to turn into a bench, which I duly did. But then I had about two feet of it left over, and it was this spare bit of repurposed wood that became the hotel. Using a variety of different-sized bits I drilled lots of deep holes into the wood, creating random patterns of tunnel entrances across the rugged old oak surface.

If the hotel had a name, it would surely be something like Sunnyside, because for the hotel to be popular it has to be in the sun. The sunlight warms the wood up, making it an attractive place for insects like hoverflies to settle on and take a little downtime, basking in the warmth. But for the red mason bee this bit of drilled oak timber is not a place for relaxation; it is a place in which to deposit the next generation. I am sitting at the table in the top part of the garden, and I have a book with me, but there is too much happening in the busy invertebrate world around me for me to concentrate on reading it. There are at least three different red mason bees going back and forth from the recycled oak gatepost whose other bit I am sitting on whilst watching them. As they come in, they hover in front of the drilled tunnels, clearly orientating themselves before they land on the surface and then dive inside the tunnel head first. Occasionally a mistake is evidently made, the bee exiting quickly, furry abdomen first, and taking to the wing once more, to hover and check its memory map once again. When the bee has got the right hole it disappears inside for around a minute, building its egg chamber within, creating a structure any human mason would be proud of, and using the mud it has carried in its large jaws as its building materials. When satisfied, it backs out into the light, before going back in again, but this time rear end first, to lay its egg.

Then it wiggles out once more and heads off to get more mud to seal the chamber, before starting another one next to it in the same tunnel. It does this until the tunnel is full of its sealed egg chambers, then it caps the tunnel entrance with mud to protect it. It is fascinating to watch, as well as very rewarding. I am watching these great little creatures, furry little bees, using something that I have made to house their next generation. It is educational as well, not only seeing how much effort the bees go to in their masonry work, but also learning directly why they take so much trouble to wall in their nesting tunnel.

Shortly after one of the bees emerges from a tunnel and flies off to gather yet more mud, a slender, dark solitary wasp lands on the bee hotel; it has beautiful yet subtle lighter markings on the sides of its abdomen that are just about visible underneath the neatly folded wings. Beautiful it may be, but I suspect that its intentions are somewhat nefarious, at least to my human mind. As it walks across the vertical surface of the wood its antennae are busy, constantly moving, sensing, as it checks out each hole in turn before vanishing into one. I don't know the species,[34] but it is clearly a parasitic solitary wasp and one that obviously specialises in these bees. It is not in the tunnel for very long, emerging quickly, cleaning its antennae and then departing, its deed done: invertebrate drama playing out right in front of me.

And there is more – more drama and more distraction. As I attempt to get back into my book I briefly look at the roses that are flowering to my left. Beautiful pink flowers adorn them, but one has an obvious white blemish on it. I look closer and realise that it is no blemish: it is a hunter lying in wait for its prey. It is a crab spider, stock still on one of the petals, its elongated front legs spread open and held back, looking for all the world as if they are a cocked trap ready to spring – which is indeed what they are. It is a beautiful creature, but I am slightly bemused by its tactics: it is lying in wait, but it is bright white sitting on a deep pink flower, so I can't help but think it has chosen the wrong flower to sit in ambush on. We have plenty of white flowers in the garden that it could sit on where it would surely blend in, with deadly effect – but choosing this one? I know I am colour blind, I know that I see the world differently to others, but even I can tell that this spider's camouflage is rubbish.

And then, as nature always does, it demonstrates that it knows what it's doing. A fly inexplicably decides to land on the petal that the spider is sitting on, right in front of it. The ensuing action is too quick for my eye to follow – a blur of movement is all I can

---

34 After a bit of research I have concluded that the wasp is *Sapyga quinquepunctata*, a species that specialises in parasitizing the Mason Bees.

A red mason bee checking into the bee hotel; the hole below it has already been filled with egg chambers and its entrance sealed with mud.

register – and then the fly is ensnared in the legs of the spider, its frantic struggles rapidly petering out as the spider subdues it. Shows how much I know.

Sitting up in the garden in the afternoon sunshine, surrounded by parasites and predators, I place my book down on the glass-topped table in front of me, its plot nowhere near as compelling as the life that is playing out all around me. As I put the book down on the glass I notice a black ant marching across the opaque surface with a purpose far beyond my comprehension. How it has got there and where it is going are questions I ask of myself, but they are questions of complete irrelevance to this small dark insect as it follows its unwavering route across the barren desert of glass. I am interested to see what it does when it reaches the edge of the table, but before it gets there to show me I get distracted and look up into the sky. Three dark sickles are scything their way through the sky above me. The swifts have returned, summer is coming, and the ant is forgotten.

Summer

The swifts slice their way through the fabric of the sky with consummate ease, aerodynamic masters of flight racing through the first heady days of summer, riding the air currents to perfection. Does any other British bird scream 'summer' like a swift? These are incredible birds, the most avian of aviators, spending virtually their entire life on the wing; if it wasn't for the practicalities of nesting they would forever fly free. When a young swift bundles out of its nest site for the first time, dropping downwards and unfurling its long narrow blade-like wings, it is embarking on a flight that could well last for years. The common swift, as our summer visitor is more formally known, doesn't breed until it is around four years old, so it has no reason to touch the ground again until it procreates. The birds are perpetual flying machines.

Swifts feed on small invertebrates, flying insects and ballooning spiders; they gather all of these from the air, exploiting the weather fronts and air currents that concentrate this aerial plankton. They even sleep whilst flying, shutting down one hemisphere of their brain at a time, enabling them to rest and recharge as they slice through the air. Constantly on the wing, they can travel well over a million miles in their lifetime. Terrestrial life is a completely alien concept to them. What a bird.

I love watching swifts, trying to keep up with them as they sear across the sky, sometimes gliding, other times accelerating hard; they trace what appear to be completely random aerial pathways, and they have an untameable aspect to them that just appeals. They are an extreme. But even though they appear to be the species most unconnected with our world, our land-based world, they are of course inexorably tied to it.

The reduction in the biomass of invertebrates in our modern world has been every bit as extreme as the swift's habits. We are losing 2.5 per cent of the total mass of insects every year.[35] Two and a half per cent doesn't sound very much, but it is cumulative, so over the last ten years we have lost a quarter of all insect mass, and in another ten it will be half of all the insect mass gone. When I was a child, only a few decades ago, a

---

35 'Worldwide decline of the entomofauna: A review of its drivers', *Biological Conservation*, vol 232, April 2019.

summertime drive would result in a smear of crushed insect bodies all over the car's windscreen, and on humid evenings it was like an invertebrate shower hitting the glass constantly. Today, there is hardly anything splattering against the windscreen, and the wipers no longer have to try in vain to wipe aside the broken exoskeletons that used to instantly weld themselves to the glass.

A reduction in insects means a reduction in the availability of food for insectivorous species such as the common swift. Less food leads to less breeding success, and that in turn leads inevitably to fewer birds. The Breeding Bird Survey run by the BTO indicates that since 1995 the numbers of common swift recorded in the UK have fallen by over 50 per cent.[36] Their numbers have halved in just that time. But it is not just the food source that is causing problems for these magnificent flyers, there is also a lack of nest sites. Swifts will have evolved to nest in rock faces, but their primary nesting habitat these days are our buildings, which are effectively the modern mimic of this habitat.

Old buildings with gaps in the masonry and under the eaves are perfect nest sites for these birds, which is why on summer evenings you often get to witness screaming parties of swifts charging around cathedrals and the like within our cities. But old buildings are few and far between, and those that exist are often maintained and spruced up without any thought to the swifts that may use them. We are constantly building new houses, and these have potential to be future nest sites, but for this to happen we have to incorporate the simple needs of the bird into the construction. It is easily done: a number of companies have already developed swift nest bricks to be used by the building industry, and their installation means that while the new house or building is still built to the modern-day high standards and is completely weatherproof and insulated, it can also provide a nest for these supreme flyers; a chance for them to raise future generations. The British government is committed to building millions of new homes in the next couple of decades, and there is no reason why every single one of these shouldn't incorporate the needs of swifts (and other birds) into their design.[37]

The swifts above the village continue to cut through the air as I watch, and swallows and house martins fly below, all of them hawking insects out of the unseen air currents. Occasionally one of the hirundines will alight on one of the telegraph wires, pausing in its activity, but the swifts of course never do; they just keep on flying. A brief snatch of the swift's screams reaches my ears. It is a shrill sound, but contrary to the normal definition it is not an unpleasant one; it doesn't jar or send shivers running through me. It is an amazing sound, and all that runs through me is delight. Somehow, by hearing that high-up bird, a connection with it is made. Screaming summer groups of swifts are something that we can never allow to be silenced.

---

36 Data from the BTO/JNCC Bird Trends Report 2018.

37 In 2019 the Conservative government committed itself to building 300,000 houses a year. Swift bricks are widely available and some developments already incorporate them, but only on a small scale. A simple change in the extensive building regulations is all that is needed for every house to have potential for swifts and other birds.

Through the gate

A beautiful summer's day, the sky a perfect panorama of unmarred blue, a day made for the moor. I drive up through the village that lies nestled above a steep cleave on the moor's northern edge, park the car and walk up the last of the tarmac until I reach the large heavy metal gate that separates our lived-in land from the unlived-in land beyond. This gate always amuses me: is it here to stop our modern life from encroaching further, or is it here to stop the wilderness from escaping its confinement? The scruffy collection of sheep beyond it make a mockery of my musings; of course, the reality is that the moor is primarily farmland as opposed to wilderness, but even so the gate is a crossing-point into a different landscape. The gate opens with effort on my part and a satisfying creak on its part, and I walk through it and onto the moor.

The contrast is immediate. The smooth consistency of the tarmac stops at the gate, replaced by a rough stony track fissured into mini-canyons by the flow of rain. The light changes too. Suddenly I am standing in bright, glaring sunshine, the trees have stopped at the gate and even their shadows don't seem to dare to cross the threshold. I am confronted with openness, an unbounded, extensive rolling landscape that reaches to the point where it meets the equally unbounded blue of the sky. The bird song changes too. Before the gate a blackbird was giving its flute-like rendition, but on this side of the gate it is a skylark that I can hear singing from somewhere high above. When I walked up to the gate a great tit, sitting in some bramble-dominated scrub, scolded me with its rolling, rasping 'Churr', but now that I have gone through the gate I am instead getting the sharp, harsh 'Chak' of a stonechat that is sitting atop a small, tatty piece of gorse. That gate truly is a gateway into another world.

I strike off the hard, stony path, taking the grassy track that heads straight up the short rise towards the military flagpole that stands somewhat incongruously in the landscape, a warning of the army exercising its right to exercise when flying red; but today no colours are displayed. At its base a meadow pipit is hunting through the tough, grassy sward, whilst beyond, in the heather-dominated ground, a male wheatear ducks in and out of view. I follow the path across the level plateau that leads to the base of the ridge I am aiming for, bisecting the old granite workings, the forgotten pits and spoil now swathed in tangled clumps of gorse, the spiky plants themselves swathed in straggly snatches of sheep's wool. In amongst the old undulations a skylark scampers, its bill already holding insects as it seeks more. Somewhere in a hidden grassy nest its chicks will be waiting eagerly for that beakful of protein.

I reach the base of the ridge, the beginnings of a granite-topped backbone that separates the Taw from the East Okement, guiding them onto their different courses that will eventually reunite in an estuary on the north coast. The twisting path that picks its way through the clitter of long-ago volcanic debris is steep and hard on the legs as it climbs steadily upwards, levelling out at the first of a chain of tors that adorn the ridge, its granite formation resembling large irregular slabs laid one on top of the other, an igneous version of collapsed Jenga blocks. I look back towards the north, over the mid-Devon plain as it extends below me, the patchwork quilt of fields and woodlands eventually blurring into a haze from which, with a strain, you can just make out the high ground of Exmoor many miles to the north.

To the west the panorama is halted by the highest ground in the whole of the South West, High Willhays and Yes Tor, forming a wall that effectively shuts out the landscape beyond it. Between this high ground and my vantage point lies the broad valley of the East Okement, the subdued hues and subtle colours of its landscape rudely interrupted by a fast-moving ribbon of dayglo yellows and oranges as a group of mountain bikers flow down the stony track that leads to the river crossing.

I ignore the distraction of the garish colours and turn eastwards, looking over the fledgling Taw towards the rounded brooding bulk of Cosdon Beacon. Above it a buzzard has the sky to itself as it traces broad circles in the air, its broad wings held in a shallow V as it rides the spiralling updraft of air reflecting off the hill. The common buzzard is still exactly that, here in Devon at least; they are beautiful birds, the eagle of the South West. The bird comes out of its soar and glides in my direction, the white marking across the breast and the dark carpal patches of the under-wings showing clearly in the light as it flies by, probably heading for the rough pastures on the edge of the moor, a habitat in which rabbits abound. Buzzards are extremely catholic in their diet, feeding on worms and beetles through to voles, mice, squirrels and rabbits, as well as any carrion they can find. Somewhere nearby, probably in the tall trees of the steep cleave that the Taw pours itself through, there will be a nest with well-developed chicks in it.

It is only a short walk along the ridge before the next collection of granite slabs forms another tor, and here, improbably, is a small rowan, somehow clinging to existence, growing from deep within a crevice between two mighty granite boulders right at the peak of the rocky outcrop. The solid granite around it has acted as a tree guard, a ring of impenetrable rock ensuring that the tree has been able to escape from the all-too-prevalent browsing of the moor's sheep and ponies. It is probably at least three years old, but it only has half a dozen leaves soaking up the sun. The rowan's leaves are highly modified, comprising of a central stem which in turn has around fifteen small leaflets growing off either side of it, with the final one growing from its tip. They look like small, serrated individual leaves, but they are not: they are all part of the one leaf. In the autumn, when they will turn from their matt green into a rusty orange colour, the stem will separate from the tree, taking the whole leaf and its fifteen leaflets to the ground as one. The bark of the tree's stem within its rocky guard is all scored and calloused as a result of the wind constantly rubbing it against the harsh, rasping surface of the unyielding stone. A lesser tree may have succumbed to this, snapping at the point of the damage, but this rowan is a survivor, taking advantage of its rocky grazing guard, despite the wounds it inflicts, and growing upwards to unfurl its leaves out of reach of the grazers and browsers that suppress its relatives elsewhere on the moor.

I stand on top of the granite that surrounds the tree's lower part. I look all around me; there isn't another tree within a hundred metres of where I am standing, and the

The granite-protected rowan growing in solitude on the high moor of Dartmoor.

odd ones that do appear at this range are of a different species altogether: hawthorns, wind-battered examples dotting the open ground. But I can't see another rowan; this small, granite-guarded tree is here in glorious isolation. I pause to consider the riddle of its existence: how did it get here, how is it that this lone tree germinated deep down in the crevice of the tor, potentially several hundreds of metres away from its parent tree? There is only one likely answer to this rowan riddle.

Rowans produce copious amounts of red berries as summer ends and autumn dawns, and these are voraciously consumed by a whole manner of birds, particularly those within the thrush family.[38] Red berries are very attractive to birds, deliberately so; the birds are the seed distribution system used by many tree species, including the rowan, to ensure that their seeds are spread far and wide. The seeds of the rowan either travel through the digestive system of the bird, protected by a hard case, or are coughed up and spat out once the bird has cleaned all the berry's flesh off it in its gullet. Whatever its route, the seed is deposited at random in a new location, often less than 50 metres from the parent tree, but it can also be as far as a kilometre away. As I look at this straggly, lonely rowan growing out of the top of a tor, it is this method of seed dispersal alone that must be the reason why it is growing here.

---

38 The second part of the rowan's scientific name, *aucuparia*, is Latin for 'bird-catching'. The berries are so attractive to birds that they were once used to bait the traps used to catch them.

Of course the thrushes don't deliberately plant the seeds of the next generation of rowans; the vast majority will fall in the wrong place and never germinate at all. If the seed which became the tree in front of me had been deposited a few inches away from where it was dropped, it would have landed on the exposed hard surface of the granite rocks, a virtual desert, rendering its chances of germination zero. Even those that are dropped in potentially propitious circumstances may find themselves shaded out, trampled or browsed. But this seed got lucky, sheltered from the extremes of the weather in this otherwise exposed location, protected from the relentless browsing of the moor's livestock, so it managed to not just germinate but also to survive. It may be a bit battered, but this rowan is a-growing.

Looking out over the surrounding moorland, I see numerous meadow pipits, a few wheatears and a couple of skylarks, all busy gathering food to raise young, but I see no thrushes. High, exposed moorland is not typical habitat of the blackbird, or the song or mistle thrush. But these are not the only thrushes that breed here in Devon; there is one more, the ring ouzel, and that is very much a bird of high moorland. Looking a lot like a blackbird with a crescent-shaped white bib across its breast, the ring ouzel is a relatively rare breeder in the UK. It is very picky in its habitat choice, breeding only in the uplands on high moorland and within mountain ranges. Dartmoor is home to a few pairs of this scarce thrush, and although I haven't seen any in the immediate area where I am standing, it is highly likely that one of them is the bird responsible for the rowan tree growing out of the tor, taking advantage of the fruits available in late August and early September before embarking on its migration southwards.

I descend down from the tour and walk across the flat grassy hump of the ridge, heading for the next rocky outcrop, with every step heading further into the moor and farther from civilisation. It is a glorious summer's day, and the land I am on is open access, open to all, yet I cannot see another person as I stride along. I'm not complaining. I love this solitude, especially in this landscape, but it does amaze me how few people ever venture here. This is as close to wilderness as we can get in southern England – it is certainly as far as one can get from our modern-day lives. Ahead of me, the imposing pyramidal shape of Steeperton Tor points skywards; behind it, dwarfing all with its looming great mass, is the ominous-sounding Hangingstone Hill, a silent, brooding backdrop. I know that at one stage I will have to turn back, I will need to head back down to the gate on the edge of civilisation. But right now I just keep on walking.

Moor to sea

The sea shimmers in the sunlight all across Lyme Bay, a huge seascape running from the tip of south Devon in the west all the way to the bulky rocky lump of Portland Bill, just visible in the haze to the east. The beach below is busy, a mixture of humanity tightly packed along the sand, some people fencing themselves off from others with brightly coloured windbreaks, others just opting for no more than a towel to declare their territory. Up here on the clifftops it is deserted; aside from a couple of cheery walkers there is no one here but me, rambling through the uncut grasses and collapsed ravines of the crumbling red Jurassic cliffs.

Rabbits graze happily on the lawns they have created close to the cover of huge bramble and blackthorn thickets, a thriving world of scrub impenetrable to humans. The somewhat hoarse scratchy warning call of a whitethroat makes me pause and study one of these wild thickets; I soon spot the bird as it hops up on to a stray branch poking out from the irregular mass of green. As soon as it takes up its vantage point its call changes to song, a brief burst of hectic jerky notes tumbling forth. The song finishes and for a moment the bird stands proud, looking large for its size, the grey head contrasting with the perfectly white eye ring and gleaming white throat from whence its rather unimaginative name stems. Then it drops down hurriedly into the security of the scrub, calling once more from its obscurity, its voice sounding like a seasoned smoker's.

I follow a random maze of grass, walled in by the scrub thickets, walking through the long unkempt grasses, some of which are collapsed, some standing proud. Many

The whitethroat, a scratchy-voiced lover of scrubby tangles. (Photo by kind permission of Peter James Carr Photography.)

times I have to retrace my steps, turning back from yet another grassy cul-de-sac, the combination of blackthorn spines and bramble thorns deterring me from trying to force my way through. Occasionally I emerge into a large open area, a secret garden tended by the rabbits, who pause in their grazing to eye me with wonder until one of them loses its nerve and thumps the ground with one of its rear feet, creating a ripple of panic as they all dash for the thorny cover. My haphazard progress eventually leads me to the site of an old collapse, a place where the red sandstone substrate has sunk down to the shore below, leaving a steep-sided gash in the otherwise flat terrain of the clifftop. This is a wild land, a margin of natural instability that separates the busy tourist-dominated seafront and coastal town from the open sea.

The wound in the landscape is an old one, and the torn terrain has repaired itself with a smattering of thin grasses, though the scrub has been so far unable to colonise the thin loose soils that remain stubbornly unsupportive of their quest. But just as I am about to step down into this geological rip I spot that something else has colonised it: at the far end of the collapse, a large tump of soil was formed by the shift in substrate, and this now-grassed mini-hill of soil has provided easy digging. In front of the large flattened oval hole at its base, sitting on the smoothly polished bare ground in front of it, are two fox cubs. Both are sitting bolt upright and both are staring with unabashed curiosity at me as I stare back at them with unabashed delight.

I am likely to be the first human they have ever seen, and not wishing to startle them I slowly edge myself backwards, lowering my profile as I retreat. Bent over, I creep away to my right, skirting around a fierce-looking mass of blackthorn, before slowly coming up to the edge of the collapse again. I lie down in the grasses and crawl my way steadily forward until the tump of soil comes into view once more. The two cubs are still sitting there, but their pose is now a relaxed one, their interest in me long forgotten; instead they are focusing on a meadow brown butterfly that is fluttering over the long grasses on the sun-exposed steep sides around them.

Fox cubs are beautiful. I don't like using the word 'cute' – surely the most overused anthropomorphic description of wildlife there is – but if anything qualifies for that dubious epithet, it is a fox cub. Triangular ears, large eyes, a soft-looking face, and that beautifully coloured fur: it is hard not to use the word when describing them. One of the cubs stretches out its darker-coloured front legs and lies down in the sun, while the other, still transfixed by the fluttering of the butterfly, ignoring its sibling's movement, is watching the insect wide-eyed. I soon discover that the cubs in front of me are two thirds of a triplet, with the third announcing its existence by suddenly bounding into view and pouncing on the prone cub, who instantly rolls on to its back, mock-fighting with open mouth and excited noises. The butterfly watcher initially ignores the rumpus going on beside it, but it doesn't resist for long; jumping up and twisting around, it too joins the mêlée of limbs and tails, giving a high-pitched yap as it does so.

The trio tumble through the grasses in carefree play that is a privilege for me to watch. Suddenly one peels away from the other two, snatching up an object that looks like the soil-encrusted remains of a rabbit's back leg. It holds it up in its mouth, displaying the trophy to its siblings enticingly, before dashing off with it, running up the steep sides of the collapsed land that forms their world; the other two forget their tumble and pursue the first, yapping loudly as they do. For a few seconds they charge around, orangey-red blurs of noise and excitement, and then the first, still carrying its prized possession, dives headlong into the hole at the base of the tump. The other two try to follow, but in a scene straight from a theatrical farce they try to do so at the same time, colliding and ending up in an ungainly heap at the entrance. One regains its composure ahead of the other and proceeds inside, closely followed by its playmate. Suddenly all is still and quiet again. All that moves is the meadow brown, patrolling the grasses around the fox's earth.

I lie motionless for some time, happiness spread wide across my face as I watch the hole intently, yearning for a repeat performance. Eventually a cub does reappear, peering out from the entrance, before padding out onto the bare soil and lying down. As it does so it yawns, showing its growing teeth clearly, and then lowers its head on to its outstretched front legs before closing its eyes and nodding off in the sunshine. There is to be no encore. I edge my way back through the grasses, get to my feet and make my way back into the labyrinth of scrub, eventually finding my way out of it, rejoining the cliff path, with a smile still wide. The path and its edges are littered with rabbit trittle – fading pellets, slowly falling apart – so there is clearly no shortage of food for those young foxes, and their mother doesn't have to travel far to find nourishment for them. To reinforce this point, a young rabbit naively wanders across the path in front of me, completely unafraid of my approach; it sits just a few yards from the path and watches me as I go by.

Another whitethroat is singing from another piece of tangled scrub, and a dunnock gleans something from the path's edge just ahead of me whilst a squadron of high-up gulls drifts by overhead; I glance back at the beach stretching off into the distance below me, its sand covered with the flotsam and jetsam of humanity. They don't know what they're missing.

Predators and aliens

I've just had a sparrowhawk fly right by me, gliding silently in behind the tomatoes, slipping over the low fence no more than 2 metres away from me, over the chilli plant I had just placed in the morning sun in my impatience for it to turn green to red. The sparrowhawk was a male, the barring on the tale exquisite as it ghosted over the young Devon whitebeam standing proudly in its pot, over the straggly, electric blue of the cornflowers, before swooping upwards under the dense hawthorn branches, losing itself in the tree's anonymity. All this happened quicker than the time it would take me to say the bird's name.

The garden has fallen silent, the constant movements and calls of the smaller birds temporarily suspended; the presence of the predator, hidden by the green cloak of the hawthorn, has paralysed their activities. I too am still, just staring at the impenetrable mass of foliage in front of me, reliving the vision of the small raptor as it glided past me.

A male sparrowhawk tucked away in the top of the hawthorn.

Then some of the leaves move, a sign that the bird has pushed up and off from the branch it was perched on. I don't see it slip out of the back of the tree, but I can trace its onward journey from the sudden exclamations of birds further down the road, its departure eventually confirmed by the harsh, angry call of a jackdaw several houses away. The raptorial spell broken, I stop my open-eyed stare at the hawthorn and look about me.

Butterflies coat the buddleia flowers: red admirals flash their bands of scarlet, several peacocks make eyes at me, whilst the more subdued meadow browns hustle for access to the miniature flowers that make up the curved purple spikes emanating from the twiggy unkempt shrub. Travelling painted ladies and small tortoiseshells move from spike to spike, and the tattered rear edge of a comma stands out amid the immaculate perfection of the others. Has a non-native invasive weed ever had such a beneficial effect as the buddleia?

We are always quick to chastise the alien, to sneer at it, even though we are, of course, always responsible for it. It wasn't the plant's fault that we introduced the butterfly bush, as it is sometimes known. We made the conscious decision to import this Far Eastern plant[39] and to cultivate it as an ornamental delight for our gardens and parklands.

---

39 The most widely cultivated buddleia is *B. davidii*. Native to China and Japan, it was introduced to Britain around 1890.

The flowers of this exotic plant are indeed beautiful, and not just to us, proving very attractive to butterflies, who flock to feast on the rich nectar within them. The problem is that all those little flowers on the multitude of flowering spikes that the plant readily produces end up fertilised, producing hundreds of seed capsules that contain countless tiny winged seeds within. It has been estimated that even a modest buddleia bush can produce over a million fertile, ready-to-go seeds every year, and it is this that makes them potentially highly invasive. While in a garden this prodigious ability to reproduce can prove mildly annoying to the gardener who finds numerous seedlings springing up all over, in the wider countryside these seedlings are seen as a potential threat to the naturally occurring flora that grows there.

But is it really such a threat? The term 'invasive plant' conjures up images of Himalayan balsam carpeting riverbanks, or rhododendrons rampaging over acidic woodland soil. Self-sown buddleias may turn up anywhere, but I am unaware of them taking over entire areas other than some urban wasteland plots, where at least they bring a bit of green to the tangle of supermarket trolleys and black bin bags dumped within. A buddleia in full bloom along a railway embankment is not just a riot of colour; it is a hugely important nectar source in a linear corridor of habitat that helps many species spread

A peacock butterfly basks in the sunlight.

into urban areas, that helps them get introduced to people who might otherwise not see them. Butterflies, including the species I can see feeding on my own straggly plant, are in freefall. The statistics about their declining populations make alarming reading:76 per cent of our species are declining in occurrence, and they are getting harder to find, they are getting rarer.[40]

Many species of butterfly adore buddleia, and many organisations, including conservation ones, recommend planting it in our gardens because of its importance as a nectar source. Gardens give us opportunities to engage with wildlife – and what is more engaging than a flock of brightly coloured butterflies feeding right in front of you? Buddleia can be an access plant; it can open the doors to the world of nature for young and old alike, who find themselves mesmerised by the beauty of butterflies feeding on it. Should we be so harsh on it?

I don't think we should be. But what we can be is careful: dead-heading the flowers once they have finished blooming stops the seeds developing, and it also encourages more flower production. Plants flower because they want to produce seed, so if those flowers are lost before it can produce any, the plant is highly likely to produce more of them. Buddleia is no exception. In response to cutting off the gone-over flowers the buddleia sends up new ones; this has the added bonus of prolonging the nectar source for the butterflies, meaning that your garden can continue to be adorned by these flying jewels right through the summer months and even into the autumn.

An old friend's lesson

The glass eye stares back at me from behind yet more glass. A small pigeon with beautifully marked plumage trapped forever in its prison of glass. It is the first of its kind that I have ever seen, a lifer, if you like, a lifeless lifer.[41] The unknown taxidermist did a good job all those years ago – at least I presume he did. I will never be able to compare this inanimate stuffed bird with a live one, because the bird in front of me is a passenger pigeon, and the only passenger pigeons left in the world are like the one in front of me. They are all dead, stuffed and behind glass, mementos of our stupidity. I am making a visit to an old lifelong companion and good friend, the Royal Albert Memorial Museum in Exeter, to see its exhibition on bird migration.[42] It is a well laid out and highly informative display with lots to engage the visitor, but the stand-out for me, the sad stand-out, is the forlorn extinct passenger pigeon sealed in its glass tomb.

The entirely avoidable fate of the passenger pigeon is well known: from millions of birds to none in just a few decades of human stupidity, blasted out of existence. The last wild bird was killed in 1901, and after that only captive birds remained. The last of these, the last of the entire species, died alone in a zoo in 1914; her name was Martha.[43]

40 *The State of Britain's Butterflies*, Butterfly Conservation and Centre for Ecology and Hydrology, 2015.

41 A 'lifer' is a birder's term to describe a species never seen before, ie the first time in your life you have seen it.

42 Birds without Borders, summer exhibition 2019. Royal Albert Memorial Museum, Queen Street, Exeter, Devon.

43 *A Message from Martha: The extinction of the Passenger Pigeon and its relevance today*, Mark Avery, Bloomsbury, 2014.

A French writer noted with alarm in 1856 that the slaughter of the birds was unsustainable, writing that it was his belief that if not stopped 'the amateur of ornithology will find no more wild pigeons, except those in the Museums of Natural History'.[44] As I stand looking at this slim pigeon, admiring its age-faded plumage and its elegant long tail, the prophetic nature of those words haunt me. Pigeons are birds that many take for granted, but they are a family of birds that have suffered badly at the hands of humans and from our actions. Because of us, at least thirteen species of pigeon have become extinct.[45] The most famous of these, the most famous of all extinct birds – an unwanted title if ever there was one – was the dodo. It was gone by the end of the 17th century, just a few decades after humans had discovered it.[46]

Only a few miles from the museum, up on the afforested hills to the south of Exeter, I used to record the numbers of a relative of the dodo and the passenger pigeon: the turtle dove. It is an exquisite member of the pigeon tribe, a dainty bird with beautiful markings and a soft purring call that seems synonymous with sunny summers, but now for me it is synonymous only with summers past. The British turtle dove population has crashed over the last thirty years. Over 90 per cent of them have vanished from our countryside, taking that beautiful purring sound with them.[47]

The sad saga is repeated in the rest of Europe as well; about three quarters of Europe's population of these small pigeons have been lost since the 1980s. They are in trouble,

A pair of turtle doves snoozing in the sun.

44 Benedict Henry Revoil (1816–1882).
45 Gill, F and D Donsker (eds). IOC World Bird List (v 9.2) 2019.
46 IUCN Red List 2012.
47 BTO press release, July 2016.

big trouble. Some think they are following the same road as their unfortunate relatives, tumbling towards extinction just as Martha and her relations did. We are told that there are several causes for this decline, but the reality is that there is just one. Us.

It is us that have altered the habitat in which the turtle dove breeds, us that have reduced the availability of small seeds in the countryside, seeds that these birds depend on for food. Seeds from wild flowers such as the common fumitory are a vital component of their diet, but wild flowers such as the fumitory are also known as agricultural weeds, and that is where the problems begin. The removal of 'weeds' from our countryside by poisonous herbicides has been one of the major factors in the steep decline of our so-called farmland birds; many species have suffered, but the turtle dove, a bird that only eats small seeds, has fared particularly badly.

Data shows that the turtle doves that are breeding in Britain today are only producing half the number of chicks per pair than the turtle doves that were breeding here in the 1970s.[48] Without sufficient food they can't produce the numbers of young required to keep their population stable. But while such a dramatic loss of productivity helps to explain the drop in population, it is not the whole story.

Passenger pigeons were shot in vast numbers for sport and for food; tragically, so are turtle doves, and they continue to be shot perfectly legally even now, when we all know that their population is crashing. Turtle doves are migratory, heading north into Europe each spring from their wintering grounds in Africa; migration is never easy for a bird, and it is even harder when they are being shot at. In Morocco, companies organise shooting parties for paying guests so that they can shoot hundreds of turtle doves a day. And then even when the birds do reach Europe this small dove is still not safe, with the species appearing on the 'authorised quarry species' list in many countries, including Malta, Cyprus, France, Spain, Italy and Greece – countries that the migrating birds pass through as well as breed in.

We know that turtle doves are in real danger of extinction. Science shows us just how many we have lost, yet we continue to allow them to be shot in large numbers. Surely we don't want another Martha. Surely we don't want future generations to know these birds as glass-eyed specimens trapped forever in glass boxes?

Caught on camera

I really enjoy putting out my trail camera in the garden to record what is happening in the hours of darkness; it is a great way of discovering species that I might otherwise not know are using it. This morning, when I put the memory card into the computer to see what had triggered it last night, I was rewarded straightaway with a hedgehog. Bumbling through the plants it went, up and over the Devon stone that demarcates the beds, then stopping to scratch in the most unbalanced of poses. I watched as it almost toppled over mid-scratch before somehow righting itself and continuing on its small scrawny legs that always seem so unlikely to support, carry and propel this rounded prickly mass. The

48 From www.operationturtledove.org .

This hedgehog is a very welcome visitor to our garden. These are mammals that need our help, urgently.

footage shows it heading off through the hebe, heading for the short section of newly planted hazel hedge, the gaps I created low down in it evidently working, allowing this nocturnal wanderer to pass from human territory to human territory.

We had always hoped that we had a hedgehog using the garden. We certainly garden in a hedgehog-friendly manner – gaps in boundaries, piles of vegetation, wild areas and absolutely no slug pellets – but we had never found any evidence of them. But because of the camera I put out, I now know that these wonderful mammals are indeed using it; they are visiting our garden, snaffling slugs as they go. Hedgehogs have suffered a catastrophic decline in recent years and whilst gardens can provide a great habitat for these night-time foragers, they can also cause problems. Aside from the nasty chemicals that we often use liberally and without thinking in our gardens, we also create barriers. Hedgehogs will travel up to 2 kilometres (about 1¼ miles) a night,[49] a distance that makes a mockery of my views on their little legs, but our habit of fencing out the neighbours also fences out the wildlife. Hedgehogs are tenacious climbers and can clamber through hedges, but when confronted with a solid wall of wooden fence they are well and truly

Summer

blocked. By creating just a small gap at the bottom of a fence you can allow a hedgehog to pass through this otherwise impenetrable barrier, giving it access both to your garden and to the garden beyond, allowing it to access and eat the slugs that can be found in them.[50]

A wood mouse briefly stars in the next video captured by the camera; something about the camera triggering evidently alarmed it and its immediate defence mechanism was to leap upwards and completely disappear from the scope of the camera lens, in fact 'leap' isn't the right word – it skyrocketed upwards, a rodent firework, removing itself instantly from the perceived danger. Wood mice are amazing jumpers; it is a great defence strategy, both alarming to the potential predator and effective in putting considerable distance between the mouse and what scared it in the first place.

I can remember when I used to monitor dormouse boxes I'd peek in through the slightly opened lid to see if it was worth taking the box down and examining it more thoroughly. If a dormouse was inside it was almost invariably asleep, and even if wide awake it was never in any hurry to leave the confines of its box.

But a wood mouse was something else; sometimes they would scurry downwards, burying themselves beneath the nesting material, but at other times they would explode out of the tiny gap I had created, rocketing outwards. We seasoned dormouse box checkers had soon learnt to stand slightly askew of the box when lifting the lid for that initial check, on many occasions I had a wood mouse fly past my ear; and once one landed square on the jacket of a colleague, disappearing inside the open zip before either of us could react. I have never seen anyone get out of a coat as quickly as he did that day!

The next clip of video shows the hedgehog returning back past the camera again; this time it comes right up towards the lens, showing its face in perfect detail as it snuffles and snorts its way along on those little legs. As it shuffles past, the spines on the mammal's back brush the housing of the camera, creating a fabulous sound – and then it is gone, exploring beyond the reach of the lens. I immediately head back up to the top part of the garden to see if I can find any visual sign that the hedgehog had been there, but there is nothing to suggest any nocturnal activity, no clue at all. Without the camera I simply wouldn't have known that I've had one of these brilliant little prickly mammals using the garden, I head back indoors and put the batteries on to recharge, making sure they are ready for when night falls again.

A safe hobby

The shadows of the trees line the track, creating a zebra-style pattern along its pale surface, a constant passage through sun and shade until the track curves around, changing its orientation, and becomes bathed in full sunlight. An emperor dragonfly zips up the side of the track, a flash of colour in straight-line flight over the verge of bracken, itself a miniature forest of single stems and dense canopy reflecting the towering Douglas fir trees that stand either side of the forest track. The conifer's sweet citrus scent fills the air,

50 You just need to make a 13 cm × 13 cm gap. Do it today!

a fresh-air air freshener. The track widens and passes a neatly arranged stack of sawn logs, the butt ends facing the track displaying the rings of the tree, the diary pages of their lives revealed to all that are literate in the language of dendrochronological history recorded in concentric circles.

Ahead, a group of fallow deer, four females and their young, slink across the open space of the track, then slip through the ferny forest and into the darkness of the real one beyond. I spot them as I get closer, their melanistic colouration allowing them to blend in well with the obscurity cast by the murky light. All eight of them have their heads up, looking at me as I walk past, watching me closely, unsure of my intentions. But my intentions don't concern deer, and I leave them standing in the shade as I continue to amble down the stony track. I turn off the main track and walk up a narrower, grass-edged path, climbing steadily up the hill. The path passes through some scrubby downy birch and a few struggling plastic-tubed oak trees that are fighting a battle with some rampant brambles that have used them as a trellis.

A large, bright orange butterfly glides along the sunny track on speckled wings before landing on the bramble; the underside of the wings show well, telling me its name as I admire the silver wash of the beautiful silver-washed fritillary. Onwards I trek, following the path as it narrows through an old granite gateway, an old reminder of the farming past of this now afforested area. After a tunnel of dark green holly the path opens out again, revealing a panoramic vista of the forest and valley below. This is where my intentions have led me, this is where I want to be; it is the perfect spot to see what I have come to see. A quick look to my left shows me that I am not going to be disappointed.

Sentinel-like, it sits on the dead pine branch on the edge of the plantation, looking out over the young trees that coat the slope below it. Even at this distance the bird's white cheeks and throat catch the sun. They always seem to sit in the sun. The hobby is a wonderful bird, a migrant falcon that arrives on our shores towards the end of April, turning up in numbers at favourite wetland sites where the bird's audacious aerial prowess enables them to refuel with ease on dragonflies and other flying insects after their long journey northwards. Once replete, the birds gradually spread out, scattering themselves across the country, returning to favoured nest sites and generally becoming much harder to find.

Now, with June in full swing, this male is sitting out on his favoured perch, looking out over his territory whilst his mate, who will be close by, is hunkered down on their brood of eggs. She will be in a nest that wasn't built by her or her mate; falcons aren't known for their nest-building, and hobby certainly don't engage in such a laborious task. They are repurposers, upcycling the old nests of birds like the crow and raven, and using them for themselves. By June, when this falcon is ready to breed, the corvid nests are empty, a resource just waiting to be used. It is a glorious summer's day, and the sentry-like falcon looks out over a forest that is alive with bird song. A willow warbler keeps popping up near to where I am sitting, its faded yellow underparts brightening considerably in the sunlight as it sings its tumbling tune. Nearby a blackcap scratches

A typical hobby nest site.

out its own song, but unlike the willow warbler it does so from somewhere within a scrubby thicket of goat willow, hazel and bramble. Further off, the distinctive bread-requesting song of a yellowhammer can just be heard, the drawn out ending hanging in the still air. There is plenty to see, but despite all the activity my eye is constantly, inevitably, drawn back to the hobby on its sun-soaked perch. Raptors always demand attention.

A few metres away from the falcon, a wood pigeon also sits out in the sun; the eternal prey of many a raptor sits unbothered in the presence of this one. Wood pigeons have nothing to fear from this falcon, a bird that is smaller than themselves and a bird that hunts smaller prey – nothing to fear at all – but they perhaps have something to gain. Many years ago I used to monitor hobby nests, under licence, for they are a Schedule 1 bird,[51] and I always found wood pigeons nesting in close proximity to the hobby. Indeed,

---

51 Schedule 1 of the Wildlife and Countryside Act. Birds on this schedule have special legal protection, and a licence is required if you are carrying out any activity that may disturb them.

the presence of a pair of wood pigeons on a promising-looking hobby site would often focus my attention on that site; the hobby can be an elusive bird, but the wood pigeon isn't.

Pinpointing hobby sites can take a while, and sitting in the forest staring out over the trees gives you plenty of time to think about things, so I would sit there and think about wood pigeons and hobbies. It turns out that many others had thought about them too, but they hadn't left it at that; they had carried out research on these two seemingly unlikely neighbours. The results of this research showed that the close proximity of breeding wood pigeons to breeding hobbies wasn't coincidental. It was deliberate.[52] The hobby has no interest in nesting, nor any reason to nest, near a pigeon, but the pigeons have a very good reason to nest by the falcon. Security.

Wood pigeons are the favoured food of many raptors, and their young are especially vulnerable, but it is not just raptors that take their toll; many of the nests fail at the egg stage due to predation by the carrion crow.[53] Hobby are notoriously neurotic parents. The immediate vicinity around their nest site is a protected space; they will not tolerate other raptors within it, nor will they tolerate crows or other corvids. Any incursion by anything that they consider to be a potential threat is met with an instant and rapid response. A screaming hobby, diving at speed and flashing its razor-sharp talons, is a very effective deterrent measure, so the area in which they nest soon becomes a no-fly zone for both corvids and other raptors.

Wood pigeons know this: they are apparently studious birdwatchers themselves, and have learnt that a nest site near a hobby is a nest site with an inbuilt security system. The research has shown that the pigeons deliberately select breeding sites near hobby ones if they can, and that these nests have a higher success and productivity rate than comparable nests that aren't near a breeding hobby.

Can birds really know? Can they really learn? We have to be always careful about anthropomorphising bird behaviour, but how else do we explain what the wood pigeon is doing when it chooses to nest next door to a hobby?

It is quite a thing to think about, and think about it I do as I sit in the sun watching over the forest. As if to reinforce these thoughts, the hobby is off its perch, gaining height with alacrity, its fast wingbeats powering it through the air, driving it upward. It calls loudly, a high-pitched 'Kew – Kew – Kew'. It is a clear warning. Several hundred metres away a buzzard is drifting on an air current over the forest below, and at the falcon's shouted warning it alters its direction – a subtle change, but a change nonetheless – and the hobby doesn't have to follow up on its verbal warning. The buzzard drifts on, heading away from the stand of pines in which the falcon and the pigeon reside. The hobby circles a few more times then drops back down to its perch to resume its sentry duty.

---

52 For example, 'Nesting association between the Woodpigeon and the Hobby', Bogliani, *Journal of Raptor Research*, vol 26, 1992.

53 'Fabulous Falcon', article on the hobby by Ian Parsons in the May 2017 issue of *Bird Watching* magazine.

Back around the village

In my childhood the spotted flycatcher was a bird of common occurrence, often to be seen in the summer months snatching a fly from above a footpath as it followed the wooded field edge, often appearing in gardens and even turning up in the public park next to my old comprehensive school. But those days are gone, and the spotted flycatcher has largely followed them. This insect-eating migrant has undergone a significant and steep decline in recent decades; since the late 1960s its numbers have dropped by about 90 per cent: nine out of every ten spotted flycatchers that bred in Britain back then have simply gone. Our background war on insects has starved them out of existence.

Spotted flycatchers are short-term visitors, late to arrive and early to go; they start arriving in May, but by late August they are already departing on their return trip to their wintering grounds again. They still come here of course – indeed, they are still found right across the country – but they are now very thinly spread. These are birds that you have to search for nowadays if you wish to see one. Five years ago I had one unexpectedly turn up in the garden; a newly arrived migrant was suddenly there in the tree opposite the kitchen door, sitting on a bare branch watching the airspace around it intently before

A spotted flycatcher intently watching for its next meal.

dashing off and snatching a fly from the air. The delight I felt as this bird returned to the branch from which it had launched itself was unbounded, and instantly my expectations were raised: would it nest in the ivy-clad wall, would it become an avian fixture of the garden over the next few months?

It left its perch again, flying up and over the hawthorn and vanishing from my sight. At the time I didn't realise that my expectations would vanish with it; but since that day I haven't seen a spotted flycatcher in my garden, not one. Then yesterday, as I turned off the main road that runs through the village and started to walk downhill, an aerial movement caught my eye. A quick darting sally from some large trees, a quick view of a small brown bird briefly hovering before it dropped back down again – a tantalising glimpse, but no more. At this point the lane runs at a far lower level than the gardens that border it, so it was impossible to see into the garden, and even though I patiently waited for several minutes, the bird didn't reappear.

Fortunately, the garden belongs to someone I know, and after a quick walk back home to fetch my binoculars I was soon ensconced in it, watching the mature trees that flank its far side, eyeing the scrubby hazel beyond that forms a boundary between the neighbouring garden and a small paddock in which two horses idly meandered about. I didn't need to wait long. Another sally, another fly snatched from the air – and there it was, a spotted flycatcher striking its characteristic pose on a broken-off twig jutting out just below the canopy leaves of a tall beech tree.

With happiness written across my face, I sat and watched and enjoyed this small brown bird as it perched on a number of similar-looking bare branches, all of which offered it a clear vantage point overlooking the garden glade below. Spotted flycatchers are not showy birds – a dull brown bird with streaky markings to the forehead and upper breast, its indistinctive features being somewhat distinctively diagnostic when it comes to identifying them – but there is so much more to the bird than just its looks. The bird's essence, the way it is, the way it goes about its day, is what makes the spotted flycatcher a brilliant bird to see and to watch. And watch it I did. For half an hour I watched its continued sorties from its various perches, I watched it hang in the air or turn acrobatically to get close to its chosen target, I watched it use its fine tweezer of a bill to pluck insect after insect out of the air.

This was clearly its space, its domain. I suspect I was watching a male bird, its mate hopefully tucked away on their nest, probably built in amongst the overhanging ivy of the shabby old stone building that the horses use as a shelter. With luck, the eggs that she is incubating will hatch, and the resulting chicks will fledge successfully. Watching the bird in front of me snatching flies out of the air tells me that here at least there is plenty of food for them.

Sitting there, watching the flycatcher repeatedly perform its name, made me feel happy. Watching wildlife, connecting with it, is a way of connecting with yourself. This bird took me back to watching a flycatcher feeding from a neighbour's apple tree when I was a child, an old recollection recalled from the depths of my mind by this bird repeating the actions of my memory bird. I can only hope that in another thirty-five years I will still be able to watch these fantastic summer migrants perform the same routine again.

The uniform green of the elm clothes the hedges along the lanes, their battered, gnarled and broken stems, the result of the crippling work of the flail, are hidden by the soft green curtain of leaves. These are the most resilient of trees, coping with the annual mechanical battering just as they cope with the ravages of the infamous fungus that doesn't originate from the Netherlands. The elms get knocked down, but they get back up again. We are told that our landscape is devoid of elms, that the trees have all been killed and are no longer – but they are still there, unless we in our wisdom have grubbed them up and burnt their root systems. If elms are gone from a landscape it is because we have removed them: if left, they survive. Just. But in nature 'just' can be enough.

The towering elms of *The Hay Wain*[54] might not be evident now, but that is because the trees are literally lying low, striving in the struggle against the fungus that has turned so many of their stems into dead wood and prompted us to clean the landscape of them; but if our cleaning were to stay above ground then the tree would have a chance to throw up new life; and if left to continue to do so then, after many generations of new growth, those giants of British art will be back.

Dutch Elm Disease, a name that comes from the fact that a Dutch scientist first identified it, has probably been locked in a conflict for millennia with the trees that give it its name. There are eras when the tree's defences dominate the fungus, suppressing it, keeping it quiet, but in between these eras the fungus unleashes a new strain, a new focus of attack, and when it does its effect is obvious to us as the mighty elm stems rapidly die. It is in one of these periods that we now live, in the eternal battle between the elms and their eponymous disease; it is the fungus that currently dominates. But it won't dominate forever.

The classification of elms is not straightforward by any means; the normal species designations are confused and muddled by the tree's ability to reproduce by cloning rather than setting fertile seed. These clones, that in the past were thought to be separate species, are now thought of as being variants of (mainly) one species: the field elm. English elm, smooth-leaved elm, Wheatley elm and Cornish elm are all variants of the field elm which have reproduced themselves clonally rather than sexually. On the face of it, it was a successful means of reproduction, but without the sexual-reproduction shuffling of the genetic pack the trees that were such a familiar sight in the British landscape were all genetically identical to one another. That left them very vulnerable to disease.

Elms have declined before. The pollen record shows that they were a dominant tree in the landscape before suddenly vanishing in about 4,000 BCE. Then they rose back to dominance once again before, around 3,000 years later, they disappeared again. Since then another 3,000 years have passed, and the elms have once again stopped laying down their pollen. Is this a cyclic process? It certainly looks like it. The modern decline started with a modest outbreak of a fairly low-virulence fungal pathogen. It was in 1927 that the

54 *The Hay Wain*, an oil painting by John Constable, dated 1821.

disease was first noted in Britain,[55] but its effects on the trees were mild. A few died, but the vast majority only lost the odd branch and soon recovered. But then in 1967 a far more virulent form of the fungus arrived.[56]

It appears that the fungus arrived on a shipment of elm imported from Canada. It soon established itself and, being easily spread by several species of the otherwise benign elm bark beetles, it proved highly contagious and raced through Britain, killing the trunks, but not the roots, of an estimated 25,000,000 trees by the mid-1980s.[57] Currently, where left to continue the battle, the tree is effectively coppiced every twenty or so years by the fungus, reducing the elm to a mere hedgerow tree, exposing this struggling warrior to the added insult of our hedgerow management.

The matt green curtain of the elms' small hairy, almost nettle-like, leaves provides plenty of cover for the sparrows. As I disturb them from their noisy gleaning of the lane's broken tarmac surface, they dive in through the green wall, continuing their loud chatter as I walk by. As soon as they judge that I have moved on far enough they are back down to the lane to continue. A male chaffinch pops up through the leaves, the light highlighting the beautiful plumage of the bird; it turns to look at me and then flies along the lane ahead, the white wing bars and white edges of the tail gleaming as it goes. It lands on top of the hedge and sings, a tumbling flurry of liquid notes, before diving back down into the very heart of the hedge, hiding in the leafy greenness of the stunted elms as I continue along the lane.

A fantastical beast of a moth, as long as my forefinger, sits unmoving on the cardboard in front of me. My identification book confirms it as the ultra-sleek privet hawk-moth. If they made moths in the 1920s they would surely have made privet hawk-moths. Pure Art Deco lines. All that is lacking is a chrome finish. This large nocturnal flyer is sitting in the morning light amongst a variety of other moths, all of whom are within the confines of my home-made moth trap. I am feeling pretty pleased with myself, for other than the bulb it has cost me next to nothing to make this somewhat inelegant contraption, and it evidently works judging by what I see before me. Armed with my field guide I begin to identify my captives, releasing each one as I do so into the cover of the leafy pyracantha hedge.

I have a couple of common marbled carpets, as well as an equally intricately marked, but much paler, silver-ground carpet; there is a very triangular-looking scalloped hazel, a sulphurous-looking brimstone similar in colour to its butterfly namesake, a wonderfully dotty magpie, and the knobbly-looking silver Y. They are all great, but none really compare to the hawk-moth; for a British insect it is absolutely huge, when its currently

55 First recorded in the county of Hertfordshire.
56 The 1927 outbreak has been attributed to the fungus *Ophiostoma ulmi*, the 1967 outbreak to *Ophiostoma novo ulmi*.
57 Data from Forest Research, a part of the Forestry Commission.

The stunning privet hawkmoth, one of our biggest insects.

sleeked-back wings are open it has a wingspan of 12 centimetres. I try to encourage it to leave the cardboard, to walk onwards into the vegetation and sanctuary of the hedge, but instead it clambers onto my finger and clings to it nonchalantly, unbothered and unruffled by my attempts to move it. Eventually it takes the hint and walks into the green cover, where it will stay the rest of the day before opening up those huge insect wings and taking to the night air once again.

Britain has around two 2,500 species of moth – a huge number when compared to the 59 species of butterfly that we have. There are no real hard and fast differences between moths and butterflies, despite the many myths (as opposed to moths), that are perpetrated, the best known of which being that moths are nocturnal. Most are, of course, but there are also plenty of day-flying ones too; in fact there are actually more species of day-flying moth in Britain than there are species of butterfly.[58]

The clearwings are a family of day-flying moths, but if you saw one you would most probably think it was something else, as these moths are mimics, and very good ones at that. They mimic members of the wasp family, from bright hornets to dark solitary wasps. They are rare and hard to find, although of course their mimicry helps them slip under the radar. Being day flyers they are exposed to insect-eating birds, and it is this that has undoubtedly led them to evolve their amazing imitation skills. The largest of them, and the most intimidating imitator, is the hornet clearwing moth. It is big, it is yellow and black, and it looks just like its fearsome namesake. It is the same size, and even flies in the same manner, as a hornet – but with close inspection it becomes obvious that it is not a hornet, as it lacks the wasp's narrow waist and has much larger, mothier, antennae. But because it looks good from a distance its disguise works; most things go out of their way to avoid close inspection of hornets.

Seasonality

58 Data taken from Butterfly Conservation website, www.butterfly-conservation.org.

I have never seen a hornet clearwing moth. I would love to, but I have seen another insect that mimics the hornet, and I have seen this one in the garden. It is the rather aptly named hornet mimic hoverfly, a sometime summer visitor to our flowers. I love hoverflies: the way they can hang on a frenzied blur of wings, not wavering from the spot they have chosen, has always fascinated me. I am not very good at identifying individual species, but I can identify the hornet mimic hoverfly or, to give it its scientific name, *Volucella zonaria*. When you first see it coming towards you its loud buzzing flight does indeed recall that of a hornet, but a closer look soon reveals it to be a fly, albeit a rather large one! It is Britain's largest hoverfly species, and is a relative newcomer to our shores, gradually colonising southern Britain since the 1940s. Its size, its flight, and the yellow and black markings on its abdomen are clearly intended to mislead. Much like the moth, the mimicry is intended to persuade predators to keep away from it, to not risk trying to eat it. The adults feed on nectar and can often be found feeding on buddleia flowers alongside the butterflies, but despite their appearance, despite the obvious yellow and black warning sign of an abdomen, they are completely harmless. However, the larvae are not so benign, although somewhat ironically they are only a problem for wasps.

If you want to find the larva of a hornet mimic hoverfly you are going to have to look inside a wasp nest, which, let's face it, doesn't sound much like a good idea. The larvae are parasites, feeding on wasp larva within the architecturally beautiful papery nests of those nemeses of summer picnics, the common and German wasps. They are an unusual case of a hornet stirring up a wasp's nest.

Standing in the lower part of the garden, my attention is drawn to the old ivy-clad wall. Somewhere in this vertical world a shrew is squeaking, a high-pitched noise just within my hearing range, and every now and then a group of the leaves twitch significantly, betraying this small mammal's movement. But tantalising split-second glimpses of something in the dark shadows beyond the glossy green leaves are all I get.

It is while I am watching the movements of the leaves that I start to notice the bumblebees. Small, dark buzzing bumbles are passing me at regular intervals, some heading for the wall and others heading away from it. Watching one of the bees as it heads towards the wall, I see it bump and buzz its way through the leaves just below the robin box that is nestled in among the large stems of the climbing plant. As it does so, another bee emerges from one leaf over; we have a nest.

I try to get a good look as they go past, trying to note the markings on them so I can identify which species we have, but the inward flights are so direct and fast that it is difficult to register the markings before the bees disappear through the green leafy veil. I can see they are small and generally dark, but I am struggling to get more detail. The exiting bees offer my best chance, but most head skywards as soon as they are free of the ivy; one, though, takes only a short flight, pitching into the blooms of one of the garden flowers in the bed below the wall. This short-distance commuter, as it crawls and flies around the multiple flowers of the plant, gives me the opportunity needed to see it in full detail. It has a bright yellow collar that contrasts with the dark body, a body that terminates in a dull red colour at the end of the abdomen. A quick trip to the bookshelf and I have identified our nester, the early bumblebee, one of our more common species. I stand just a metre away or so from where the bees are busy in and out of the ivy leaves; they all fly by me, around me, without any concern, and my presence causes no reaction. Like all bumblebees, the early is a gentle creature.

Up in the top part of the garden, I am sitting on the wooden bench enjoying a cup of tea when my eye is caught by a sinuous rivulet of shimmering copper which flows across the broad smooth surface of a stone before it enters the folds of the dark waterproof material that covers the barbecue, vanishing from my view. I wait a few moments and then carefully peep into the folds – and there, loosely coiled as always, is this coppery delight, a male slow worm, refulgent even out of the sunlight. Unwittingly, in choosing the cover for the barbecue we had also selected a brilliant basking site for this legless lizard, a basking site that this male readily and regularly enjoys. In fact, he spends more time enjoying the barbecue than we do.

He is quite used to my nosiness and ignores my inquisitiveness. Occasionally flicking the air with his black tongue he remains otherwise motionless, absorbing the warmth radiating from the sun-soaked material around him. He is a good size, around 40 centimetres in length, a fine adult specimen and hopefully a voracious devourer of slugs. Slow worms love eating slugs; they should be every gardener's friend.

The garden on this fine warm summer's day is a hive of busy activity. Away from the three-dimensional bumblebee highway and the basking lizards, there are young sparrows wing-fluttering, begging for food, trying to convince their parents that they should be fed next. The sheer effort of their rapid wing movements threaten to topple them off the wooden fence that they are just about perched on. They still have that fluffy appearance to them that is typical of all newly fledged birds, and the yellow at the side of the gape is visible even with their bills shut. There is no let-up in their demand for food; every move of their harassed parents is followed eagerly. One of the youngsters decides it can't wait on the fence any longer, opting to beat the queue of its siblings to intercept the food delivery. It makes its move, flying strenuously and a little uncoordinatedly across the patio to join the adult female foraging in the herb bed. It is immediately rewarded with a feed, which leads the other youngsters to follow suit, a haphazard flight that results in one of them misjudging the altitude required to clear the stone wall of the bed and landing on the face of it, then sliding ungainly down to the ground from where it calls plaintively. The adult hops up onto the stone and looks down at the youngster, but she ignores its calls, and instead of going down to it she returns to the herb bed to continue her search for food. The young sparrow sits for a few seconds on the patio, contemplating the wall before it, and then it is up and over it using a combination of flight and scramble. Dignified it isn't, but effective it is. It lands amongst its siblings and immediately starts fluttering its wings in solicitation.

There are young birds in all parts of the garden; the blue tit chicks have now fledged and seem to spend their days pinging around it at a reckless pace, their yellow-washed juvenile plumage making them readily identifiable. They are still getting fed by their hard-working parents, but in the last few days I have noticed them exploring the branches of the trees and shrubs themselves, scrutinising them carefully and pecking at any potential food that catches their eye as they progress down the road to independence.

The blackbirds are gathering mealworms in their bills again, a sure sign that they have yet another brood of young to feed on what must surely be the last stage of this year's breeding conveyor belt. The tatty plumage of the female, an overt symbol of her hard labour, makes her as readily identifiable as the male with his leucistic spots. These are our blackbirds, boldly feeding on the scattered food as we sit on the bench watching them, their innate wariness of humans broken down by their nestful of begging young. The female in particular is not shy when it comes to getting the food her young require; if there are no mealworms to be found she comes to the back door and calls, attracting our attention to the lack of food outside.

We don't mind her demands – in fact we delight in them. The pleasure she brings us as she shares our space is indescribable, and for us watching her gathering the soaked insect larvae just inches from where we sit is a privilege, a connection with nature right on our doorstep, a connection that makes us feel that everything is right with the world. We even talk to her.

The female blackbird will come looking for us if her supply of mealworms runs dry.

⁎ ⁎ ⁎

If trees could talk to us they would surely do so in wise words. Their experience of life spans several of our own lifespans; they have witnessed much, they have endured much. But would we listen? I doubt it. Sitting in the shade of a tree on a summer's day can inspire profound thoughts such as these; under the canopy of leaves your mind is free to wander, and mine does as I sit beneath a large open grown oak. I guesstimate its age from its girth, probably around 300 or 350 years; this is a tree that could have germinated as we restored the monarchy after Cromwell, a tree that had pullulated from an acorn as the Great Plague and then the Great Fire raged in London.

As I look up from beneath, I can see from its form that this is not a survivor from a long-cleared woodland; instead, its large, strong limbs radiate out evenly from the stem, forming a rounded, consistent crown. This isn't a tree that has grown in the company of others; it is a tree that has grown alone, a tree that has grown out in the open rather than in a woodland. Acorns are heavy seeds; they aren't borne by the wind like the seeds of some species. When a ripe acorn departs its cup on the tree it falls directly downwards; it doesn't land out in the open, but within the shadow of its parent, where if it even germinated it would struggle to grow, eventually becoming a narrow-crowned individual rather than a well-rounded one. This tree, then, is a tree that was planted.

But who planted it? It is of course impossible to tell, but the odds are that this tree wasn't planted by a human; if I was a betting man my money would be on this tree being planted by a bird. But not just any bird. I'd wager that this tree was planted by the feathered forester, the jay. The jay is an unusually colourful corvid, a beautiful blend of pinkish grey, bold black and white, and an electric flash of blue on the wings; it is a truly stunning bird, but it isn't, sadly, a showy one. Jays are normally shy, preferring the obscurity of woodland to the more open habitats of their more familiar relatives, they are also innately wary of humans and for good reason, for there are some that persecute them mercilessly, even today. Jays are omnivorous in their diet, eating a wide range of items; in the spring they will predate the nests of other birds – it's what they do, it's their ecological niche at that time of the year – but come the autumn, when the fruits of the oak ripen, their diet becomes very much centred on acorns.

It is fair to say that the jay loves acorns, but as with most seeds these parcels of nutrition are only available for a short period of time; for just a few weeks of the year acorns are abundant – there is a glut of them on the feeding market – and for those few weeks the jay eats little else. Corvids are well known for displaying behaviour that we would recognise as intelligence, and the jay is no exception; they don't just feed on the acorns but they also lay them down in stores, provisioning themselves with their favourite food throughout the forthcoming winter months. These are birds that plan ahead.

They are voracious gatherers of the oak's fruits: one European study revealed that in the four-week period when acorns were available, sixty-five jays stashed a staggering

The jay is a spectacular bird that is also rather good at planting acorns.

500,000 of them. In the UK it is estimated that every single year jays cache 1,500,000,000 acorns. One and a half billion! That's a lot of acorns.

These colourful birds collect the acorns from the tree before flying some distance away from it. They can carry up to five acorns on each journey, four in a special pouch in their gullet and one in their bill. They travel with this load to the site that they have selected to stash them in. They are picky about where they stash their acorns, very rarely choosing one in the shady depths of woodland, preferring to opt for open habitats instead – open habitats just like the one I am in now. They are wily birds, alert that others may be watching what they are doing and where they are hiding their winter stores. To cut down the risk of their food being consumed by others they avoid putting all their eggs into one basket; each acorn is individually hidden, with the bird taking great care in how it does so. It will dig a hole in the ground and place the acorn into it before covering it back over again, and will then do the same for the next acorn of its load, this time selecting a site around a metre and a half away from the first. Once its cargo of five is hidden, it will return to gather more. And so it goes on.

Jays are very careful with their acorns. They don't damage them in any way; they are certainly caching acorns, but you could also say that they are planting them. As I look up through the sprawling canopy above me it is likely that this massive tree was planted by a jay. Of course the jay's actions are about securing a food supply, but given the numbers planted it is hardly surprising that some locations are forgotten, or that the birds may perish in poor weather or be killed by predators before they can recover their stores. Unwittingly, jays have become the mechanism for oaks to spread; any oak growing in open country is likely to have been planted by one. The trees don't need us humans to propagate them, they already have a long-established relationship with a bird that does that.

We consider a species to be native to Britain if it was here prior to the land bridge with the Continent disappearing under rising sea levels at the end of the last ice age, approximately 10,000 years ago. We have two species of oak that are native, the pedunculate and the sessile; they are very similar to one another, and to most people they are just the one species, the so-called 'English oak'. As the ice sheets retreated across Europe ten millennia ago, trees followed them northwards, and those that were able to distribute their seeds far and wide – trees like the silver birch, which can release a million tiny windborne seeds a year – kept a pace with the retreating ice and the virgin land underneath. But those like the oak species, with big heavy seeds, couldn't keep up; they could only inch their way northwards every twenty or thirty years.

Except they didn't inch their way northwards; they kept up with the species that had small windborne seeds. They didn't get left behind; they too raced after the ice sheets. The pollen record shows us that the oaks advanced at a far greater pace than they should have been able to. The oaks were obviously getting help, and the jay is the only likely candidate. A jay will often carry acorns hundreds of metres away from the tree it gathered them from – one was even recorded carrying acorns over 20 kilometres (about 12½ miles) from the parent tree before it stashed them. Think about how many generations of oak there would have to be for the tree to advance 20 kilometres if there was no jay to carry the heavy acorn for them. But with the bird's help this can be done in just one generation. The ice sheets retreated northwards, opening up open, unshaded land to the north – the very open space that jays still select today to plant their acorns in.

Without the jay, the oaks – our oaks – would not have got across the land bridge before it was swamped by the rising sea. We would have no native oaks, and the fabled English oak would never have existed. Our landscape would be very different indeed. Perhaps the whole nation's history would be different without the oak that built our navy and the ships of the empire …

Sitting in the shade of an oak on a sunny summer's day can be a relaxing experience, but if you allow your mind to wander and wonder about the tree you are sitting beneath, if you allow yourself to think about how it got there in the first place, the experience can quickly become mind-blowing. It is thanks to a jay that cached an acorn on this site hundreds of years before I was born that I am able to sit in the tree's shade today. It is thanks to the jay that we have oaks at all. We perhaps owe the colourful corvid everything.

The swifts have gone and their shrill screams have become a memory again; now their sickle-shaped wings are slicing through the air to the south, getting further away every minute, vanishing from our skies until next May. It will be nine long months before the screaming dasher returns. Swifts are one of the last birds to arrive here to breed, and they are also one of the earliest to depart.

But not all migrants are in such a hurry.

High above me, as I look upwards from the garden, I see aerial gangs of adolescent hirundines revelling in their newly fledged freedom, chasing themselves across the sky, dashing through the medium that they are beginning to master. Despite their height, I can still hear the swallows twittering, and the martin's drier, more throaty, call, as both species feed up and fly on, building up their body weight and flight muscles ahead of their own migration later in the year. They are a pleasure to watch, mesmeric in their movements. I relax as I watch them in the sky above the village, the young hirundines unwittingly becoming my visual stress ball. Their graceful weaving movements are all that occupy my mind; watching these birds, immersing myself in them leaves no space in my head for other thoughts. What the birds above me are doing is undoubtedly important for them – the flight skills and the muscles they develop now will help them in the months ahead – but what they are doing is also important for me: they are my nature fix for the morning.

The bright blue sky of the morning in which the young swallows and martins are roaming degrades rapidly into a heavy grey blanket of rain-laden cloud that seeps across the skyscape from the west. Summer rain is coming, and as the front advances so the hirundines switch their flight activity, the high-up hawking of insects becoming a contour-hugging chase as the arriving low pressure drives the flying insects downwards, forcing their predators to follow. Suddenly there are obstacles to be negotiated in their protein pursuits, but these graceful flyers adapt to the change in circumstances with consummate ease. The humidity builds in the air and the swallows fly lower, skimming the grasses at what seem like reckless speeds. The rain will interrupt their flying, bringing an unwanted break in their ability to catch food, and a prolonged spell of rain now could have a profound effect on the success of the next brood of youngsters bunched hungrily in the mud-pellet nests in the vicinity.

When the rain comes later in the afternoon it falls heavily and relentlessly, grounding all hirundine flights, restricting the air traffic to a few hardy corvids and the occasional mealworm-seeking blackbird. But after a few hours it eases up and gradually peters out, allowing the swallows and the martins to take to the air again in the late evening, feeding themselves and their young in a frantic bout of activity before the coming darkness grounds them once again.

*Swallows flying low over water, gathering insects
as they put on weight ahead of their migration.*

The river that bends itself sinuously around the village now runs brown, the slow, pellucid flow of yesterday transformed overnight by yesterday's rain into a fast-moving rich chocolate colour, the water of the river now loaded with the earth from the surrounding farmland, washed off the recently ploughed fields and straight into the watercourses. No margins are left to intercept the field's soil; the plough lines run as close to the streams that feed the river as the tractor driver is willing to go. The result is all too plain to see: the soil's goodness flows beneath me, washed out and away by the rain. The agricultural industry doesn't mind, though. More taxpayer-funded money can be spent replacing this natural goodness with chemical fertilisers that soon too will find their way into our watercourses, paving the way for more to be purchased and used, and ultimately wasted.

In contrast to our wastefulness on the land, the hirundines are once again airborne, slicing effortlessly and efficiently through the air, maximising the opportunity to feed, to develop their young flight muscles, or to provide for their second brood. They have no slack in the system, no bailouts to sustain them if they fail to sustain themselves. We can learn a lot from birds.

National contradictions

I am utterly alone in a land of contradiction. I am standing in an open landscape overlooking the birthplace of the River Exe. I can see no one. The occasional vehicle on the black line of tarmac several hundred metres away behind me is apparently the only link to the human world, except that the landscape I am standing in is completely and utterly humanised. The

A land of contradiction? The treeless forest above the source of the River Exe on Exmoor.

high moor of Exmoor National Park, its soft rounded hills missing the jagged granite teeth of Dartmoor further to the south, is thought of as a wilderness landscape, except there is nothing wild about it. To many people I am standing in a landscape immersed in nature – but much of the nature that should be here is long gone, lost.

I love this place. It feels good to be here, yet its reality makes me sad. It is a place that feels atavistic, but there is nothing primeval about it. Around me the landscape looks wild and untamed, but in stark contrast to how it looks, this is a landscape that is unwild and very tame.

It is a story repeated throughout the uplands of Britain: much of our supposed wilderness areas, often celebrated as national parks, are simply not wild. They are broken habitats, overgrazed wastelands, sheep-wrecked landscapes, as one writer so memorably named them.[59] The vast open expanse of Exmoor in which I am standing is beautiful to the eye, a cherished landscape for locals and visitors – but we should never think that it is natural. It is in fact a treeless forest, a desert of biodiversity; it is just that we think, we believe, that it is natural and wild. National parks were not set up to be natural areas, but over time we have fallen into the trap of thinking that this is what they are.

There are no trees anywhere around me, not one. This lack of trees is not natural. The tree line in Britain is around 600 metres above sea level, and I am standing in a place that is between 400 and 450 metres above the sea, well within the natural wooded zone. If this was truly a wild area, a wilderness, then the Exe Plain and the bare Brendon Hills around me would be a mosaic of three-dimensional habitat, a wooded tangle alive with life, a mixture of wet open areas, scrub and woodland.

The uplands of Britain are overgrazed. Sheep and deer are the grazers, and it is we humans that are, of course, the culprits.

Looking out across the treeless forest spread around me, I can see lots of white blobs grazing away any chance of arboreal resurgence; they are joined by the darker shapes of red deer, four of whom, within a hundred yards of me, are ambling across the hillside; they don't appear to have any troubles, no aim in their wanderings, no focus other than browsing and grazing. They also have no predators – predators that would focus their minds very sharply indeed. Exmoor as a landscape may look wild and untamed, but Exmoor, like everywhere else in Britain, is a landscape without its apex predators. And a landscape without its top predators is a landscape adrift, lost, lacking, broken.

There are no wolves, no lynx, to keep the deer on their ungulate toes, but if we are to think of these areas as being natural, as being wilderness, then they should be here. They are meant to be here. They are the regulators of our ecosystems, maintaining their health, keeping them functioning. But as soon as you mention bringing back species such as the wolf and the lynx, nature becomes a very emotional subject, debates instantly become vociferous, and opinions become polarised. But the sad truth is we extirpated these native predators, and as a result we broke the country's naturalness.

59 George Monbiot in his eye-opening book, *Feral*, published by Allen Lane in 2013. A must-read.

In doing so our wild woods of our uplands have become overgrazed, nutrient-poor grasslands, maintained by unsustainable, heavily subsidised sheep farming and an artificially high deer population. It is a tragedy. But what is even more tragic is that we now think that these landscapes left behind are wild and natural. I am standing in a land of contradiction, a place I enjoy coming to, a place that I love and respect, a place that is beautiful, a place that feels free from the pressures of everyday life. I want to be here, to be in this landscape. Yet when I think about it I see it for what it really is, and that hurts.

I walk through the uniform grasses, watching the occasional meadow pipit flash the white edges of their tails as they bounce in and out of the vegetation in front of me. A beautiful golden-ringed dragonfly powers past me, the dry chitinous click of its four whirring wings easily audible as it does so. It lands on a bent grass stem to soak up the sunlight, its wings held out flat and at right angles to its exquisitely marked body. It is one of our biggest insects, and is a species that needs this open moorland, a species that may well benefit from our altering of the natural landscape. Seeing it brings me pleasure, makes me happy. Yet more contradiction.

The golden-ringed dragonfly.

Roe and river

A harsh, curt bark resounds through the sultry summer evening air. To those not familiar with it the sound could easily be mistaken for that of a dog, but this is no dog barking: it is a deer, a male roe deer. As July blends into August so the roe rut gets going; and now, a couple of weeks into the latter month, the breeding season of our smallest native deer is beginning to come to an end. Even though it is now highly likely that the females of the area will have all been mated, the males are still highly aggressive and highly territorial, so the bark that I heard will have been one of these males. It is somewhere close by.

I try to lure the buck into the open with an imitation of the female roe's squeaky call, a call she uses to attract males to her. It is she that initiates the breeding. My attempt is poor, but I am hoping that the buck will still be interested, and hoping that the testosterone flowing through his system will be enough to cloud his normally shrewd judgement. But there is no obvious reaction, although a robin looks at me curiously from a branch nearby. So I try again, scaring the robin away but not seemingly getting a response from the buck, which has now gone very quiet.

I wait a few more minutes, standing on the field edge, looking towards the small brake of woodland from where I think the bark emanated. Nothing – no bark, no movement. I turn around to head off in another direction, when I glimpse through the forlorn gappy hedge beside me a roe buck standing in the next field. He is staring right at me. He is probably about 70 metres away, I hold my pose; roe deer don't have the greatest of eyesight, and with the hedge partially screening my shape I am confident that he hasn't detected what I am. I try my feeble squeak again, instantly getting a reaction from the buck, who holds his head up higher, his large black nose urgently sniffing the air, sifting the olfactory dimension for the one scent he so eagerly seeks. He is puzzled by my probably poor imitation of a female; he is unsure of what to do, and so he stands his ground, looking at me, using his ears and his nose to try and work out what's going on. His short spiky antlers on the top of his head shine in the low evening light, his moist nose glistens; but still he remains indecisive.

After a few moments he starts to walk towards me, a steady gait across the field. Now it's my turn to make a decision, but just as I am about to do so he stops abruptly, sniffs the air again, turns tail and bounds off across the field, barking loudly as he goes. He must have picked up on my scent, and I guess from his reaction that I don't smell alluring enough for him. I wait for him to vanish from view before I move off, feeling pleased with myself that my roe doe impersonation actually worked, but unsure as to whether the buck I saw was the one I'd heard. Roe are shy deer, mainly solitary and not forming the herds that other species do, so they can be hard to detect, and many people don't see them even though they are widespread across the country. It could well be that a second buck was present, but if he was he remained characteristically elusive.

As the sun dips lower, closing in on the western horizon, a song thrush starts up its tautologous song, prompting a wood pigeon to attempt an accompaniment of a more sonorous nature: two very different songs that seem to meld in the fading light.

A roe buck moulting its winter coat in preparation for the summer rut. (Photo by kind permission of Stuart Gillies.)

Back home I rush to set up the moth trap. The light is no longer fading – it has gone – but the sky is still bright enough for me to see what I'm doing, and it is also bright enough for others to see what I'm doing.

On the telegraph pole that supplies our phone line a tawny owl is sitting motionless, the light from the uncurtained bedroom window enough for me to see that the bird is watching me intently. Owls always seem to watch you intently, and now the bird's wide eyes are staring blankly in my direction as I stare back at it. The brown owl performs a slow deliberate blink, and as it opens its eyes again it swivels its head downwards and to the left, turning its intent stare to what lies below it.

I no longer hold interest for it. I head back down the steps into the lower part of the garden, past the honeysuckle which instantly envelops me in its rich intoxicating night-time scent, and when I reach the back door I look back towards the pole. The owl is still there, still watching the space below intently.

The alders flanking the river cast a thick, heavy shade over the equally dark water that hardly seems to flow; columns of gnats come in and out of view as their summer dance takes them in and out of the sunlight that has in places somehow penetrated the green mass of tree leaves above. The warmth of the summer day creates a sleepy air as I sit out on the grassy bank in a gap in the trees, basking in the sunlight; everything seems to be at leisure, and even the buzzard circling in the blue sky above me seems to do so with an indifferent air.

A male banded demoiselle damselfly is patrolling the sunlit part of the river in front of me, a glorious insect with a metallic body whose colours seem to change as the sun bounces off it, confusing colours for my colour-blind eyes, but spectacular ones nonetheless; I might not be able to name the colours but I can see their beauty. It hovers a short distance from me, showing the dark, fingerprint-like mark on its fast-moving wings, and then it zips off again, dashing downstream, before pausing to hang in the air once more.

I look back to my left, peering into the shadowy tunnel that the trees have created over the river, and to my surprise I spot yet more vivid colours. I hadn't been aware of its arrival, but about 30 yards upstream from where I have been sitting for some time a kingfisher is sitting motionless on its perch, its dagger-like bill pointing downwards as it watches the water below with a fixed stare. The kingfisher is a jewel of a bird, an avian delight. It is facing upstream, clearly showing me the vivid blue of its back as it stares downwards. Its perch is a record of how high the winter waters of the river reach: it is a long thin stick that got itself jammed in amongst the sprawling roots of an alder as the water rushed past, but those waters have long since dropped and the stick has been left high and dry, maybe about a metre and a half above the current summer level. The stick may be stranded, but it is a perfect perch for the king of fishers.

The bird suddenly moves its head. It is a slight move – no more than a small tilt, really – but it is noticeable. Just as I am wondering whether the bird has spotted a fish it answers my thoughts by suddenly dropping off the perch and diving headlong into the water, creating a splash of disturbance on the flat calm surface. The sudden action in this soporific setting is over so fast; even before the water droplets thrown up by the impact of the bird have dropped back down again to reunite with the river, the kingfisher is already heading up to its perch. The dive was as successful as it was brief, and the bird sits on its stranded-stick perch with a small fish held firmly in its dark bill. The fish is moving, but the bird soon stops its struggles, smacking the fish's head against the stick in a sudden violent movement. With its prey now very much subdued, the kingfisher juggles it in its bill until the fish is held head first, and gulps it down with an exaggerated action. The bird sits there for a about half a minute more, allowing its meal to slip down whilst the ripples of its dive dissipate below, and then it drops off its perch once more. But this time it does so with a blur of wings as it flies bullet-straight away from me, the glorious electric blue on its back like a tracer bullet zipping through the darkness of the tree tunnel.

With the kingfisher's departure, life on the river bank resumes its languid state, only interrupted by a passing charm of goldfinches living up to their collective noun as they twitter their tinkling call across the valley. I watch the demoiselle perform its aerial antics as it feeds and patrols along the stretch of a more open section of river to my right;

it is impossible not to admire its flight skills, as it makes incredible turns and Mach 3 accelerations.

I start to think about breaking the soporific feel, start to think about getting up and heading home, when my ears pick up on a babbling series of ringing whistle-like calls coming from the tops of the alders. With a quick shift of position I soon see the source, a small flock of acrobatic birds hanging off the very tips of the tree's uppermost branches. They are silhouettes, the bright sky behind them making it impossible to make out any colours or plumage detail. But I know what they are. Their small shape, with the typical V-shaped finch tail and their collective chatter, as well as their extreme nimbleness as they feed on the slender ends of the tree, are all the characteristics of the siskin.

Siskins are brilliant little birds, brightly coloured finches, all yellow and black contrasts, with a pretty, babbling vocabulary. They are fairly common, but by spending their time in treetops they often go unobserved – or if they are seen, it is often as they are now, small dark shapes against the sky. Occasionally in the winter they will come to feeders, bringing their exotic looks right into your garden, I have known many a casual bird lover be confused by this bright yellow little bird as it feeds on their seed feeder, and I have had many conversations where I have been doubted when I have suggested that the bird in question is actually a common native bird, not some visitor from afar.

The siskins that I am watching in the trees remain silhouettes, only very occasionally giving me a tantalising glimpse of the yellow as they move from tree to tree, feeding busily. I wait where I am in the hope of a more colourful show – they may even come down to the water for a drink – but it appears that I have already used up my allotted birding luck for the day on the earlier kingfisher, and when the siskins eventually move on I follow their example and head for home.

It is late August, and the summer ebbs slowly away. Redshank and black-tailed godwit form feathered masses on the marsh, and in amongst the many are the few: a green sandpiper, a ruff and a couple of spotted redshank. A grey heron stands motionless, head tucked in, perhaps sleeping off a large fish. The marsh is alive with birds; a living feathered undulating blanket covers large parts of it, and the numbers are building up every day as new birds arrive to join the others. Leaving the grassy marsh behind, my friends and I move further off down the lane before reaching and then climbing the steps to look out over the mudflats that are becoming vaster in their size by the minute as the waters recede, a kingfisher zips along on a blur of rapid wings bringing a blaze of vibrant colour to the grey-brown mud, a blaze that even the reflected sun off the wet estuary mud fails to burn out.

White blobs of little egret dot the scene; a few decades ago their presence would have caused a sensation, but now they are merely noted, passed over as other birds are searched for, from the exotic to the everyday. Their expansion and recolonisation of old haunts has been rapid; it was only in 1989 that they were recorded in Britain in any number, a small influx of wintering birds, some of which stayed on. The first confirmed breeding took place in 1996,[60] and now the number of breeding pairs is over 1,100, whilst in winter there are as many as 11,500 of these elegant white birds sharing the colder months with us.[61]

A line of Brent geese fly overhead, gargling their flight call as they go, the heavy, ponderous flap of their wings audible in the still air. Avocets, graceful pied splendour – the bird equivalent of 1920s elegance – sift the shallow waters overlying the rich silt, their upcurved bills filtering out tiny crustaceans as they sweep them, metal-detector style, through the water. Oystercatchers, distinctly stocky in comparison to the dainty avocets, probe their carrot-like bills higher up the tideline. Teal waddle in the mud, pushing their bills into it as they too filter out sustenance from within. Sweeping the binoculars across the mud, I suddenly find myself performing a cartoon-style double-take, retraining my optics onto a bird I have just swept past. My first impression is one of complete puzzlement, as the bird looks like some sort of white-headed oystercatcher – and then I realise that is exactly what it is. To give it its official title, it is an aberration, which is an unfair label for a bird that just looks different from the more typical of its kind. It is an oystercatcher that is exhibiting partial leucism; in other words, like the male blackbird in our garden this is a bird that has white bits where it shouldn't.

Variation in bird plumage is the norm, but the variation is normally so slight that we don't necessarily notice it,[62] but in this bird it is obvious. Its entire head and neck are completely white when they should be black, so it gives the bird a completely different appearance to the other oystercatchers around it; but the longer I look at it, the more I realise that it is still an oystercatcher, with its dumpy appearance and bright orange bill. We all watch it for several minutes, each one of us jokingly claiming we have discovered a new subspecies.

We depart the elevated viewpoint, still laughing and joking, and walk around the lane that loops along the point of land at the confluence of the two estuaries, before emerging onto the side of the larger river, the Exe. The mud is now well exposed by the ebbing tide, leaving only a central channel of flowing river water. There are waders all over the mud: ducks and geese abound and herons and egrets stand proud on the mud, whilst all along the high-tide strand line gulls and crows work the debris diligently.

From nowhere a peregrine powers past us, a blur of potency scattering a bow-wave of panic across the low, receding waters of the estuary. Birds take to the air everywhere in a mass feathery panic, but all are discounted by the predator amongst them – all but one, that is. The unfortunate chosen one. A black-tailed godwit is the target, but the bird stubbornly refuses to get up from the water. One, two, three attempts to get it to fly, to get it to enter the air, the arena in which the falcon excels. The peregrine cannot risk striking

---

60 BTO BirdFacts, Little Egret.

61 'Population estimates of birds in Great Britain and the UK' Woodward et al. *British Birds*, vol 113, 2020.

62 Birds also see in other light spectrums (ultraviolet) that we cannot. Just because we see two birds looking identical, it doesn't mean that to a bird they do.

it in the water; to do so would risk this supreme aerial hunter hitting the water itself, and its feathers would not cope with the immersion that may follow. Its aerial prowess would be useless against the fast flow of the river, so it has to get its prey in the air, into its medium. Once more the falcon rises, gaining height and then stooping at reckless speed, making an impossible turn inches above the water, swooping head on towards the wader, a deliberate intimidation designed to frighten, to force the bird into flight. But the godwit holds its nerve and stays low in the water, and all the aerial master can do is flash its talons at it in a futile, frustrated gesture. The godwit stays within the sanctuary of the water, and the peregrine is disappointed.

As we watch, spellbound by the spectacle, various people politely pass by, oblivious to the life and death drama playing out on the estuary in front of them. 'Birdwatchers,' one of them says in a knowing way, just in case their companions were not able to work it out for themselves.

With the thwarted hunter departing the scene, the waders return to the mud and the receding waters. Both they and calmness descend once again. There are more birds to come; their breeding season in the far north finished, they are once again on the move. The arrival of the waders and the ducks portends the arrival of autumn.

Autumn

Autumn dawns with a hunting hornet, a sonorous buzz as she flies between us, ignoring our efforts at gardening as she hunts the flowers in the beds and the leaves of the goat willow above them. The apex predator of our garden's insects, the hornet comes with a fearsome reputation in human tales, but in reality she is completely indifferent to us. She is gathering food for the now-doomed nest, helping to raise another generation of the yellow and black hunters before they succumb to the relentless change of the seasons. But before the nest declines, new queens will emerge. Huge, fearsome-looking wasps that in reality are gentle, unobtrusive insects, they will mate with a male and then seek a hibernation site, spending the winter slumbering away before emerging in the spring to found a new colony.[63]

The deep buzz of the predator fades away as she dashes beyond our garden in her characteristic straight-line flight; to our eyes there seems to be plenty of potential prey in the garden. The flowers are awash with various hoverflies, flies and bees and wasps – but nothing caught the compound eye of the hunter, and so the voracious vespa flew on.

A speckled wood butterfly basks on the render of the cob wall, a delicate decoration in the September sunlight; a peacock, more exuberant and brash in its colouration, follows suit, using our cottage as a vertical sunbed. The calendar may have turned over into meteorological autumn, but there is still a summery feel to the garden. Many of the garden flowers are still in full bloom, the bees still buzz, the hoverflies continue to amaze me with their aerial skills, and there are still several young birds around the garden, including a young blackbird that has learnt from its parents that we are a source of mealworms. Young blackbirds are beautifully marked, and at this stage it is impossible for us to tell whether the bird is a male or a female, but we know it likes mealworms because when we open the back door it will invariably be sitting on the wall of the herb garden waiting for us. If the door is open, it will boldly walk in to attract our attention,

---

63 Queens and males are produced in the autumn; they will partake in a nuptial flight before the males die and the females seek a hibernation site from which they will emerge in the spring, usually in April.

The young blackbird, relaxing in the early autumn sun and waiting for more mealworms.

heading back out of our house again as calmly as it entered so we can feed it at its spot on the wall. Earlier in the year we enjoyed watching this bird's mother when she came to us looking for mealworms, and now, as autumn dawns, we find ourselves deriving great pleasure from our interactions with one of her youngsters.

Yes, there is still a summery feel, but there are signs that the times are a-changing. The hawthorn berries are swelling and becoming more obvious amidst the leaves, ripening redder each day, a future promise of a feast for the mealworm-obsessed blackbird and its siblings as well as the many other thrushes that will soon be with us. The days are getting shorter and the year is slowly beginning to wind down.

Autumn arrives and leaves

Late September and the sun is shining, a beautiful blue sky and short-sleeve temperatures, the proverbial Indian summer. As we walk around the short, unimproved turf we are surrounded by people and by rooks and by stones. Big stones. Stonehenge is an iconic monument. We might not know exactly why it was erected almost 5,000 years ago, but we flock to it in our masses – as apparently, do the rooks. Most of the human visitors are busy taking photos of the stones, or photos of themselves in front of the stones. I'm watching the rooks.

It is not that common to get really close to these gregarious corvids – they are wisely wary of us humans – but around the stones of Stonehenge they seem happy to mix with us. One sits on a fence post and babbles away *sotto voce* as we stand watching it from a distance of 2 metres at the most. At this close range you really get to see the amazing iridescence of the bird's plumage, the normally dark blackness of them completely transformed into a dazzling array of colour that confuses my colour-blind eyes. I might not be able to put a name to the colours I am seeing on this seemingly talkative bird, but that doesn't matter; they are simply beautiful and need no label to be enjoyed. The rook on the post continues its soft vocalisations, whilst others swagger across the short turf and yet still more cut across the blue sky above. The short turf and the fact that this land has not ever been farmed intensively make Stonehenge an attractive feeding location for these invertebrate-loving corvids. There are not just archaeological riches in this soil. To prove the point a rook is digging at the ground beyond the rope that separates the humans' path from the standing stones; it is on its own dig, using its large, heavy bill as a pickaxe to break through the turf. Once through the turf, its bill switches from being a blunt pick into a delicate extractor, and we watch it carefully pulling out an inch-long insect larva from the soil, eating it quickly and hopping away from its excavation as another rook flies in and lands by it, eager to see what the first has discovered.

The short unimproved turf of Stonehenge is a mecca for rooks, some of which undertake their very own excavations.

There are people and rooks all around the stone circle. The birds have evidently learnt that the predictable clockwork flow of people around the monument poses no threat to them, but instead provides an opportunity. As soon as someone peels off from the circular flow and settles down onto the grass, a rook will sidle over to take a look, and if that person then proceeds to remove something from a bag, the rook shows more interest. These are birds that have learnt that the humans here are a food source that can be exploited.

Many humans oblige, tossing pieces of sandwich towards the birds; it's great to see people interacting with these corvids, especially as it may well be the first time that some of these people have ever seen a rook close up. What a great place to have your first interaction with one! It is interesting eavesdropping on the conversations around us; people are noticing the birds, some are laughing at their waddling stride, and many are calling them crows – something that the pedant in me wants desperately to correct – but they are all enjoying their presence. Smiles follow sandwich tosses, happy faces watch as the rooks eat the bread, people laugh at the bird's rough calls, and some even try to mimic them. It is clear that interacting with wildlife is bringing pleasure to the visitors of Stonehenge.

Later in the day as we head back down the A303 it feels very much like a summer's afternoon; the sunglasses are on as we follow the sun's progress west and the windows are open to cool the car's interior. But there are clear signs that summer has passed and autumn has already arrived. The sunshine and the temperature may fool us, but they don't fool the trees; for them the autumnal processes are already well under way. The A303 is an old travel route that in places dates back millennia,[64] but much of it was realigned and dualled in the early 1990s with new sections built to cope with the increasing volumes of traffic using it. With the new expanses of tarmac came planting schemes on the verges and embankments: many thousands of saplings were planted. These saplings are now trees, and as we drive along it would appear that many of these trees are field maples.

Field maples are beautiful: our only native member of the large Acer genus, they are often overlooked. Earlier in the year, and when you are on foot, their smaller size and uniform of uniformly green leaves help them to merge into the background. But come the autumn and they become noticeable, even when you are driving along a dual carriageway.

All along the new sections of road, the leaves of the field maples have turned a beautiful yellow; there are clumps of them dominating some areas, and at other spots there are individuals glowing amongst the greens of the other tree species, but wherever I look I see them. The maple's autumn colour is a far more reliable indicator of the season than the unseasonable weather.

---

64 The part of it that runs past Stonehenge is believed to roughly follow the route of the Harrow Way, an ancient trackway that dates from around 500 BCE.

Autumn is famed for the spectacular show of colour produced by deciduous trees; the turning of the leaves from green to yellows, oranges and even reds is widely celebrated and often commented on. It is something that largely passes me by, though, as the colour palette of reds, greens and oranges is not one that colour-blind people are all that good at defining. I still see the changes of course; it's just that I see them differently and perhaps less obviously, than others do.

It is inevitable each autumn that somewhere in the media there will be a headline talking about the show that nature is putting on – but of course it is not a show in the true meaning of the word. It is a process, a process in which a deciduous tree prepares itself for the rigours of the winter to come. Its leaves contain a variety of chemical compounds, and these compounds are often coloured. The dominant colour for most of a leaf's life is of course green, and it gets this colour from chlorophyll, the dominant chemical compound present within its narrow confines. Chlorophyll is a vital chemical for leaves, as it is responsible for driving the process of photosynthesis, converting solar energy into the chemical energy, the sugars which fuel the tree's growth.

During the spring and the summer, the tree is constantly producing enough chlorophyll to ensure that this process works perfectly; as it gets used up within the leaves, so it gets replaced. But when autumn arrives in our temperate zone the production of chlorophyll in a deciduous tree slows and then stops, and as the chlorophyll already in the leaves starts to degrade, the tree starts the process of reclaiming and recycling the chemical compounds within the leaf. As a result, the green colour of the leaf starts to diminish, or rather it starts to be diluted.

There are other compounds present all year around in leaves, and these have their own colour; but it is only as the chlorophyll degrades and is reabsorbed that the dominant green gets weaker, and it is then that these chemical compounds and their colours come to the fore. The two main remaining players are the flavonoids and the carotenoids, chemically coloured yellow and orange respectively; they too are degrading and being reclaimed by the tree, but the process for them happens at a slower rate, meaning that in the interim their chromatic influence becomes noticeable to us. Although they were always there, we couldn't see them, their presence masked by the dominance of the green.

Whilst this colour change is going on the tree is producing cells that are literally cutting off the connection between the leaf and the twig, and as this happens so various sugar compounds produced by the breaking down of the other chemical compounds become trapped and concentrated within the leaf. Depending on a variety of conditions – prominently, but not exclusively including the weather over the late summer period – these sugars start to produce another chemical compound, anthocyanin. It is not really understood what role is fulfilled by the anthocyanins produced in the leaf, but it is thought that they help protect the leaf and therefore the tree itself from harmful chemicals. Whatever its role is, its presence is very noticeable, for it is this compound that colours the leaves purple and red. (It is anthocyanins that are also responsible for the colour of the skin of aubergines and for the colour of fruits such as blueberries and blackberries, as well as the colour of red cabbage.)

Not all trees produce these anthocyanins; some have leaves that are dominated by flavonoids or carotenoids, and others are a mix. This is why we have a mixture of hues on display in the autumn, as opposed to a uniform blanket of colour. The change in the leaf colour signifies in nature that change in the seasons is happening; it is a chemical process that the tree undergoes to prepare itself for the winter months and the weather that those months bring with them. But it is supposed to be quite a show nonetheless.

Our native trees aren't restricted to colouring up the autumn with just their leaves. Fruits too provide the opportunity for colours to be displayed, but one native does this far more spectacularly than any other – although, as with many of our native trees, it is a species that isn't readily known. It is one of those trees that we seem to be tree-blind towards, although I don't understand how. The spindle is a common enough tree, a

The fruits of the spindle add a splash of exotic colour to our hedgerows and scrubby areas in early autumn.

component of woodland, hedgerows and scrub across the country, and at this time of year it is hard to miss, decorated all over with bright pink Chinese lanterns. But miss it we often do.

The beginning of autumn is when this tree is at its visual finest; while its leaves are turning from green to red it is the fruits that really catch the eye. They look exotic; they look like they belong in the ornamental gardens of a stately home – and indeed you can often find them there putting on a show surrounded by the finery of the heavily landscaped beds in which they have been planted – but they also grow in scruffy hedgerows, just as the one nearest to my house does. The fruits are in two parts: bright orange-cased seeds that are themselves encased in four-lobed fuchsia-pink lanterns that hang down amidst the leaves, a showy autumnal wonder. These autumn fruits are delicate in structure and beautiful in colour. But the show isn't for us; it is to attract birds, to entice them into eating the fruit and spreading the seed. The seed passes through the bird's gut harmlessly, but if we were to eat them these seasonal beauties would poison us. It might not quite be up there with the yew in its toxicity, but eating these pretty fruits will make you very ill, perhaps even lethally so. The spindle's beauty is certainly one for us to enjoy, but only visually.

During the Second World War, the tree acquired the unwelcome tag of being a potential threat to our national security, a tag that threatened its very presence in our country. It had nothing to do with the toxicity of the fruits, though; it was all about an aphid called the black bean aphid. You might not have heard of that name, but if you garden you will know it, as its other name is simply blackfly. This small species of insect can do damage to many food crops, including – as its more formal name suggests – beans. Being a native tree, the spindle plays host to a whole variety of insect species, one of these being the aforementioned aphid, an insect that has the potential to impact food production. Back in the 1940s, with concerns at the time already high about the nation being able to feed itself[65] there was real concern that an outbreak of the black bean aphid could cause real problems. The spindle does indeed play host to the aphid, and it was therefore decided that the best way to combat any threat was to eradicate the spindle tree from our countryside. It seems bizarre to think that this was considered, but considered it was, and plans were even drawn up to carry it out.

Aside from the obvious fact that to completely eradicate a native and widespread species of tree would take a huge budget and a massive amount of manpower at a time when both were in short supply, there was no consideration of the fact that the spindle plays host to not just aphids but a wide variety of insect species that predate these small sap-sucking insects. The tree's spectacular fruit is also highly attractive to birds, many of which will also eat aphids. You could easily argue that the spindle actually helps keep the dreaded black bean aphid in check; after all, a healthy ecosystem with all components intact tends to be a balanced ecosystem.

---

65 On 5 November 1940 Winston Churchill made a speech to the House of Commons urging the nation to think ahead and to think about endeavouring to produce as much food ourselves as we could. This speech was then used in the famous Dig for Victory campaign.

Thankfully the order was never put into action, as there was already scientific evidence that was able to show that whilst the aphids do indeed use the spindle, they don't actually need it to be present. These tiny insects drift over from continental Europe every year as a type of aerial plankton – the very plankton that high-flying swifts can be seen hawking way above our heads on clear summer days. The removal of one of our native trees would have had no effect whatsoever on the aphids and their potential depredations of our food crops – indeed, it would have probably exacerbated the problem by the removal of a tree that plays host to, and provides food for, many of the aphid's natural predators.

I walk past spindle trees growing in the hedges around the village on most days. They are easy to overlook at most times of the year, but now, as autumn embarks, it is a tree that is hard to miss; the colour of the leaves and the amazing fruits of this otherwise unassuming tree are beautiful indicators that the seasons have rolled on once more. This is a tree that should be noticeable not just for its autumn spectacle but also for its amazing back story, a back story that should be a salutary lesson to us all when it comes to making decisions about our countryside.

The yellow leaf lets go, tumbling down through the other leaves, through the branches, before catching in the hard stiff spiky leaves of the holly below. The autumnal cascade starts slow, but once begun it cannot be stopped. The process that sees the trees jettison their coat of green has the rather formal-sounding name of *abscission*: the tree withdraws itself from the leaf before cutting it adrift, and down it drops, the inevitable fall, as autumn marches onwards.

The process of trees dropping their leaves has always fascinated me; as a child it seemed such an extreme thing for a tree to do, abandoning such a fundamental part of itself, although of course, like most kids, I revelled in the drifts of dead crunchy leaves, wading through them with glee. Not every tree contributes to the autumnal cascade, but those that do so do it for a reason, and that reason has nothing to do with entertaining young children. Deciduous trees lose their leaves to conserve their resources as they head into a period of torpidity; they also do so to reduce the risk of damage from strong winds. Large, broad leaves catch the wind just as sails on a boat do; the surface area exposed to the movement of air on a fully leaved tree is vast beyond comprehension and when the surface of those leaves is wet with rain the effect is multiplied. Winter is the time of stormy weather, strong winds and rain, so to continue through this period covered in potential sails is to risk limbs and even life.

But not all trees go through this process: most of the conifers of course keep their leaves, but these leaves are much, much smaller, and shaped so that not only does the wind pass through them far more easily, but also rain can't accumulate on their surface. There are, of course, some broadleaf trees that aren't deciduous; they keep their leaves all year around. Probably the best known of these non-deciduous broadleaves is the holly.

The holly is a prickly character, and is probably the one tree that everybody can identify with ease. It is evergreen, but it is not reckless – nothing in nature is reckless. The leaves of the holly are thick and shiny, adapted to avoid losing water, to preserve resources that are lost through the more typical leaves of other broadleaf species. They are still vulnerable to strong winds, but the holly is typically a tree of the understorey, mainly growing in woodlands, keeping its head down, letting the other species tower upwards, allowing them to raise their heads above the parapet.

The holly is *dioecious*, a botanical word that in simple terms means that they are either male or female, a concept that is easy for us mammals to comprehend but one that is unusual in our trees. This is the reason that some holly trees bear the famed red berries and others do not: those with the fruits are female and those without, male.

The holly's leaves are dropped and renewed, of course, but it is a gradual process spread over years rather than a season, and it is something that happens individually rather than collectively. The thick leathery leaves can stay on the tree for up to five years; the holly is an economical tree. Its thriftiness is also apparent in the shape of the leaves: Hollies are well known for their spiny, spiky leaves. The sharp needle-like spines are there to protect the tree from greedy browsers, and they are effective at doing so, they

When browsing pressure is no longer an issue, the leaves of the holly often revert slowly to a spineless oval shape.

are a response to browsing pressure, but browsers can only reach a certain height and once the tree has grown tall enough to be out of reach or the browsing pressures relents, its leaves begin to lose the biologically expensive spines, reverting over time to a more simple, more economical, oval shape.

The berries on the holly in the woodlands around where I live are numerous this year, a promising larder for the many birds that feed off them as well as a promising resource for Christmas wreath makers. There is a quaint traditional tale of how an abundance of berries on a holly foretells a hard winter, the tree producing a weather prediction for us to interpret. But the red berries are no weather forecast: they are in fact a weather report, a report that dates back many months, back to late spring and early summer when the holly was in flower. Both the male and the female trees produce small yellowy-white cruciform flowers,[66] and for there to be berries in the winter the flowers have to be visited by insect pollinators. A wide variety of bees and flies pollinate the holly, so if the weather conditions are conducive to insect activity when the holly is in flower, then the berry crop in the winter will be good, but if the weather is poor – if there is a period of wet and cold weather as spring turns to summer – then the berry crop will be reduced. The holly tree foretells nothing. It can only tell you what has been.

To wit is to woo

Craneflies dance across the kitchen windows, a silent ballet over the surface of glass, irresistibly drawn to the light from the darkness of the garden. Up and down the panes they dance on their delicate wings and impossibly frail legs, but inevitably some fall foul of the traps set. Forlorn struggles follow in tangled webs, the long legs of the daddy long-legs snared at severe angles as the spider wraps its newly acquired prey in unending silk.

From the impenetrable darkness beyond the life and death drama being played out on the glass, comes the two-syllable call of a female tawny owl; she is close to the house as she calls again, but cloaked in her blanket of darkness she remains invisible to us in our brightly lit kitchen. She is answered by a male, his softer, quieter reply much more distant. The two calls amalgamate, forming the characteristic 'Twit Twoo' sound forever associated with these birds.[67] The female is likely to be sitting upon the telegraph pole in next door's garden, watching the path below that separates one earth bank from another, an open space that is crossed regularly by the many small mammals of the garden. Sometimes if I venture out of the back door at night I see her dark silhouette drop off the pole, vanishing quickly into the gloom of the shadows below.

The tawny owl is our most numerous owl species, and whilst generally associated with broadleaf woodland they are also quite at home in an urban setting; they can be found hunting voles in city cemeteries just as readily as they can be found hunting them

---

66 The flowers of both sexes are similar: both are small with four white petals, but while the male flowers have four yellow stamens at their centre, females have a single style.

67 Many people think that the twit-twoo call is made by a single bird, but it is actually a combination of the female calling and the male responding.

in remote woodland glades. As long there are trees to nest in and prey to catch, the owls are not necessarily fussy about where they live. There are estimated to be about 50,000 pairs of tawny owl in Britain.[68] They are supreme nocturnal hunters, using their acute hearing to locate their prey.

Owls have asymmetrical ears, with one ear located higher up on the head than the other; the ears are also slightly different in size, and positioned at different angles to one another. It is a configuration that would look odd on a human, but these ears are of course hidden beneath the head feathers of the owl. The differences in position and structure of the ears means that the bird's brain receives the sounds that it hears through them at slightly different times; we are talking fractions of fractions, but that miniscule difference enables the bird to precisely pinpoint the source of the noise it hears. It is always difficult to compare abilities, but it has been estimated that the tawny owl's hearing is ten times more sensitive than our own. Even in total darkness, if a vole moves below it, the owl will know exactly where it is. Owls have good eyesight, their disproportionately large eyes enabling them to utilise all the light available, but they don't have night vision. It is hearing that is their number one nocturnal sense, not sight.

The female outside is using her hearing to communicate with her mate, who may be several gardens away. The pair bond is strong in the tawny, and these birds use their distinct calls and good hearing to maintain contact during the dark nights. They are also advertising their hold on the territory, warning other prospecting owls that this piece of land and sky is already taken. Autumn sees an upturn in their territorial behaviour; the breeding season may be in the next calendar year, but the female I can hear calling to her mate will be laying her eggs towards the end of January beginning of February. For us, autumn marks the quiescence of the year, but for our brown owls the breeding season is on the cusp of starting once again. We stand at the window, making no sound, as we listen to the communicating owls somewhere out in the darkness beyond.

Harvesting the fruits

I return home with purple-stained fingers, the age-old signature of blackberry picking. There is autumnal abundance to be had, and this year there is a bountiful harvest of blackberries, big juicy fruits packed with fibre, Vitamin C and Vitamin K. The seeds, when not getting annoyingly wedged between your teeth, are also good for you; packed full of fibre, they are also a source of omega-3 and protein.[69] Pies and crumbles are planned for some of the haul, but the majority are destined for glass bottles: once these are full of the glossy black fruits, gin and a little bit of sugar is poured in over them to create a treat for next year. Blackberry gin, damson gin, sloe gin,[70] I enjoy them all and enjoy making them, just about managing to have the patience to leave them for a year

---

68 'Population estimates of birds in Great Britain and the UK', Woodward et al. *British Birds*, vol 113, 2020.

69 From an article 'The Health Benefits of Blackberries' published on the BBC *Good Food Magazine* website.

70 These are simple drinks to make yourself: steep the fruits in gin with some added sugar for anything between 3 and 12 months. The sugar not only sweetens the drink but also thickens it. A quick search of the internet will come up with a ratio of how much sugar to fruit.

before filtering and decanting, and then it's all about the enjoyment of tasting last year's wild flavours on a cold winter's night.

Blackthorn trees, the source of the sloe gin we made this time last year and that we will soon be enjoying, are beasts of the arboreal world. Don't let the pretty white blossom that lightens up the dark unleafed tree in March fool you; they are, as mentioned earlier, aggressive land grabbers, returning open ground to scrub, preparing the way for and sheltering the bigger trees to come. Spiky, spiny tangles of branches ready to rip clothes and skin, the blackthorn is prepared to defend itself in its quest of recolonisation.

When at college all those years ago, I and my fellow student volunteers spent our Wednesday afternoons trying to prevent these spiked gatecrashers from establishing themselves on the fragile chalky grasslands of the North Downs in the county of Surrey. Armed with bow saws and loppers, we would seek them out before doing battle with them. I still seek them out, but nowadays only to take note of their location in preparation for this time of year, when the sloes ripen into their purple-sheened glory. When I first started making the dark alcoholic delight of sloe gin over twenty years ago, I studiously followed the lore of old, waiting to gather my sloes until after the first hard frost, when the icing of the fruit's flesh released the sugars within, reducing their harsh astringency: early October would see me out, eagerly plucking the tiny plum-like fruits from the dark spiny branches.

But now I can't pick them at the beginning of October; if I still followed the old rules the sloes would be left behind on their twigs, waiting for the autumnal frost that

Freezer-frosted blackberries ready to go from autumn fruit to winter tipple.

never comes. In recent years, the first frost has arrived so late that the sloes themselves have already passed: either they have been plucked off the thorny tree by others or their velvet-like sheen has been replaced by white mould as the fruits begin to degrade in the now mild and damp autumn weather. To make sloe gin nowadays in the South West of Britain, I need to employ a freezer instead of a hard frost to sweeten the fruit; in an ironic twist – I need to use energy to counteract the effects of climate change.

As I think back to what were great afternoons on the North Downs, I do so with a heavy dose of irony. We were conservation volunteers, helping the rangers and wardens that managed the nature reserves, gaining knowledge and experience whilst doing our bit. But our task, in simple terms, was to stop nature being natural. We were conserving what were essentially artificial habitats, interfering with natural processes, stopping the land from going back to its natural wild state. The work we carried out benefited rare butterflies and other invertebrates, so it certainly had its conservation value in that respect, but the rarest of invertebrates in Britain depend on deadwood, the sort of habitat that exists when you let land go back to its natural state, allowing nature to manage itself. Conservation in Britain is a bit like gardening; we don't like letting go, we feel that we need to manage things ourselves, wanting sites to look like how we want them to be rather than how they 'want' to be. There is, of course, a place for these managed conservation habitats – chalk downland and lowland heath are valuable habitats supporting some special species – but should we in the name of wildlife conservation manage them against natural processes? It is a conundrum, especially in the limited space that wildlife has in Britain. Thinking about it, it is enough to drive you to drink, which is where the sloes and the blackberries come in …

I take a short drive around the lanes that lead north from the village, meandering along the narrow tarmac strips that are hemmed in by steep banks and flailed hedges, before parking the car in a small layby and getting out. I look down the lane in front of me. It doesn't look any different to the few miles I have just driven along – a car's width of tarmac flanked by the banks and the hazel and elm-dominated hedges on top – but there is something else here, something special. I walk a few hundred metres along the tarmac, enjoying the weak warmth of the sun above, until I come to a spot where there is some shade cast onto the lane, the shadows of two small trees, and it is under these two that I stop.

The two trees are growing either side of a telegraph pole, their unknowing aid in escaping the flail. The one on the left is an ash, a common tree in most of Britain, but the one on the right isn't so common. It is a Devon whitebeam. It is a tall, thin-stemmed and straggly-looking tree, but its leaves look healthy, and more importantly so do its fruits. I use an old rabbit hole in the bank as a foothold and stretching to my limit I manage to grab a cluster of the orangey-brown fruits; some are still hard but a few have started to blet, and these fall apart in my hand as I grasp them.

Back down on the lane again, I examine my collection; eight of the fruits are still firm and I put these in my pocket, but four of them have bletted and their flesh has smeared itself across my fingers and palm. I pick the dark seeds out and put them in a small paper bag that I have brought with me for this very purpose. I then proceed to clean my hand by eating the fruit's flesh off my skin. Standing in the middle of a lane and licking your hand may not look dignified, but there is no one about, and besides not only does it do the job but it also tastes delicious.

The fruits of the Devon whitebeam resemble mini-apples in shape. Before they blet they are hard and not very flavoursome, but once the bletting process begins the flesh softens and sweetens, to produce a real foraging treat. Their texture is grainy, like a pear, but they are much sweeter than these more familiar fruits. I absolutely love them. Perhaps I ought to try them with gin?

This tree on this lane is the parent of the Devon whitebeams I have growing in my garden, and of the many other Devon whitebeams that my friends and relations have growing in their gardens too. The Devonian's tree deserves to be in Devonian gardens, and over the years I have done my bit to ensure it is in many! I am sure I don't need to germinate more seedlings next spring. I am sure that I don't really have the space for yet more young trees – but I am also sure that when I get back home the seeds in my paper bag will be placed in some soil and put safely away in the cloche.

The fruits of the Devon whitebeam.

It is tempting to take more of the fruits, but it is not just me that enjoys them; the thrushes and the blackbirds eat them, and I have even seen jackdaws helping themselves as well, somehow hanging on to the thin branches and managing to keep their balance by flapping their wings as they pluck the berries from the tree. Any that are dropped during the bird's endeavours will provide food for the voles and mice of the hedge bank, small mammals that are very partial to the fruits of Devon's tree. Looking about the rest of the hedgerow, it is clear there is little else in the way of fruit for wildlife to eat; the hedge has been relentlessly flailed, and the trees within, with their brutalised stems, can't produce the fruit and seed that could sustain so much. The fruits of the Devon whitebeam and the seeds of the ash are an oasis in an ironic desert of food-producing farmland.

A cold morning start, my breath visible as miniature wispy clouds in the still air. There are beads of glistening dew on the vegetation around me, crystal-clear drops hanging from the ends of twigs. It is time for the emergence of old friends – the hedgehogs, the penny buns and the deceivers, to name but three. There are of course many others – many, many others – and some of these are to be appreciated with a note of caution: poison pies, panthers and even death itself. Mushroom season is here again, the time of year when the normally hidden world of fungi suddenly literally explodes out of the earth in a multitude of forms and colours.

There are many words written at this time of year on the reappearance of these fruiting bodies, that seem to magically form overnight. Much is said about their edibility and their toxicity. Sometimes their graceful forms elicit articles, sometimes their crude shapes elicit mirth, but what I love more than anything about the world of fungi are the epithets that we have given them. I love the appellations, the monikers, the labels, the titles, the names we give to the myriad of life in the fungal world. The fungi kingdom is a huge one, and some of its inhabitants don't yet have an English name, but there are many that do. And what names they have.

Out there on this cold morning awaiting my keen eye, there is an A–Z of wonderful names, everything from the aniseed funnel to the zoned tooth. Some are bluntly descriptive – the death cap does what it says on the tin – but others are subtle delicacies of names: angel's bonnets and shooting stars, names that conjure up fanciful images. I could find myself with a pink disco amongst the beech trees, and if I'm lucky I might share a salmon salad with the old man of the woods or see a tiger's eye staring back up at me.

There are so many evocative names for the fungi that surround us, yet many people are blind to the diversity of fungal life; some are even scared of it. For them there are only two types: mushrooms which come in cellophane-wrapped packages, and toadstools that will kill you without warning. There are of course some fungi that are very poisonous – the aforementioned death cap will indeed kill you – but these are very much in the minority, and even the most deadliest of death caps can only kill you if you make the decision to eat it.

I enter the wood, the first part of which is dominated by widely spaced grand old Scots pines, their needles carpeting the floor below, with only occasional clumps of bilberry and some straggly forlorn-looking heather breaking the monotony. I spot my first fungi almost instantly, standing upright with their caps looking wet and shiny, I recognise them from some distance away: slippery jacks. These relatives of the more sought-after boletus mushrooms are common under pine, their distinctively ringed stems and glistening, slippery caps making them an easy fungus to learn. There are other fungi dotting the surface of discarded pine needles – yellowy caps of the ochre brittlegill, formerly known as the common yellow russula, are abundant – but both these and the jacks are not what I am looking for.

On the side of the narrow ribbon-like path that I am following is a beautiful silver birch, its pendulous branches drooping gracefully. Already its leaves are rich with their autumn hues, contrasting with the white and black combination of its bark. I run my hand across the smooth white parts of its stem, feeling the moisture on its surface, and strike off from the path, walking with deadened footsteps across the soft floor of needles until I come to a large old earth bank that separates the pines from a stand of towering beech trees.

I scramble over the bank and into the very different world of the beech woodland. There are no needles here to deaden the footfall, just swaths of dry, brown and very crunchy leaves. Being colour blind and foraging for fungi is, perhaps, not the safest of combinations, but the fungus that I seek is unmistakable, even for me. The woodland floor is a complex mix of autumn browns, where leaves cast dark shadows upon more leaves; it is a disruptive pattern, but even it can't hide the small bright purple mushroom I am looking for. It doesn't take me long to find some amethyst deceivers; a small troop of them are poking up through the thick leaf litter just a few metres in from the bank, their colour unlike anything else on the woodland floor.

When the fruiting bodies are young and fresh like these, they are unconfusable; it is only as they age and weather that they start to deceive, changing colour and becoming harder to identify. I gather a few of them, plucking them from the layer of beech leaves by their thin stems. They are of course edible; they have a faint mushroomy taste, and although they are not in the gourmet class, it is their vibrant colour that makes them a great addition to a meal, giving it another dimension. I have enough, and leaving in place the many other troops that I spot to continue studding the brown floor with vibrant colour, I turn my attention back to the bank and walk along its steep flint-flecked sides.

I spot my first hedgehog close to where a large beech tree is growing out of the top of the bank, the tree's clasping roots dropping down the bank side and into the soil below. But the hedgehog I see is not of the mammalian type, it is a white undulating-topped mushroom growing out of the side of the earthen bank. As I approach I see several more of varying sizes scattered about the roots of the tree. These are gourmet-class mushrooms, firm-fleshed and full-flavoured. There is some minor slug damage to the cap but nothing serious, so I pick a handful, leaving the smaller specimens to develop. They get their name from the underside of the cap; instead of gills or pores they have tiny little spines pointing downwards. As the colour of the deceivers is distinctive, so are these spiny structures, allowing me to pick them with confidence.

Further along the bank there is more white catching the eye; but these are no fungi, they are feathers, the soft downy feathers of a wood pigeon. There are more feathers – primaries and secondaries as well as the characteristically marked tail feathers – scattered around the bank, and as I look up into the tree above me I see more downy white feathers hooked on the moss growing along a large horizontal branch. A perfect plucking post for a sparrowhawk. It seems as though I am not the only forager here.

I duck back out of the wood, content with my small haul, and walk down the lane. The sunlight has started to dry the dew off the hedgebanks, but in the shade the spider webs still hang, adorned with little refracting pearls of water, and a breath of a breeze is flowing down the lane carrying with it tiny fluffy seed parachutes hoping for a propitious landing: the last of the hedgerow dandelion clocks are winding down.

Deer

Autumnal spider webs capture the crystal-clear autumnal sunlight, glinting deadly treasures decorating every gorse bush lining the meandering sheep path across the moor. The air is fresh, and I am conscious of its chill as I breathe it in. Above me a buzzard ascends on a sky-tightening spiral, following an invisible thread upwards, deep into the blue. What a day, what a *glorious* day.

Picking my way through the myriad ovine pathways that criss-cross the ground, I find myself by a perfectly shaped mass of granite; it's not very big, but it is invitingly formed to be sat on, so sit on it I do.

I look to the sky. The buzzard is no longer in view; either it has become a miniscule dot in the bright blue above me or it has drifted off along the fast-moving high air currents, the evidence of which can be seen in the few small fluffy white clouds that are scudding across the otherwise open sky. Where I am sitting, the air movement is no more than a tickle against the face, but higher up it is a rapid river.

From nowhere, a honking arrowhead of Canada geese appear, the laborious flapping of wings audible even above their incessant voices. They are crossing my skyscape, heading roughly north-west. As I watch them, the neat shape of their formation falls apart and for a few seconds they are flying in a chaotic jumble before they reassemble themselves into an uneven V shape, looking more like an upside-down tick of approval than the sleek arrow of before.

I get up from my hard seat and continue my walk, deciding to head for the far-off tor on my right-hand horizon. Surveying the land in between me and the distant outcrop, I note the change of colour in the vegetation, the telltale change from faded pale straw to

Seasonality

100

vibrant green. I arc myself up the slope and around the wet mire that lies in my way. The diversion lengthens my walk considerably, but it comes with the bonus of maintaining dry feet, something that is always important on the moor. As I near the tor, walking up the steepening sunny slope, a late and very tatty-looking meadow brown butterfly flitters past, apparently enjoying its last days even if on ragged wings. I watch it for a few moments as its bumbling flight takes it away from me out across the open expanse, before I crest the ridge on which the tor broods. A handful of meadow pipits are feeding on invertebrates, picking around the short turf at the base of the tor, taking advantage of the overgrazed terrain that lies on the leeward side of the rocky outcrop. The sheep of the high moor are a hardy bunch, but their grazing patterns produce a telltale map of shelter from the prevailing weather.

I clamber up the collection of large grey granite slabs that make up the tor, my boots, despite being slick with moisture, gripping the rough textured surface of the igneous rock with ease. From the top I spot a kestrel, pressed hard into the air, gripping it with its wing beats, as it scours the ground below for food. Turning around, I spot a pair of ravens, flying in wide-spaced formation, their flight slow and languid as they move across the moor, watching all that is happening below them. Sheep dot the ground, insidious shearers subtly shaping the terrain, removing any arboreal colonisers before we even notice they are there.

A darker movement catches my eye on the opposite side of the shallow valley from where I stand on my rocky viewpoint, I can see it's a red deer, but it is only with the help of my binoculars that I can see it's a young male, his single-tined antlers betraying his immaturity. His journey through the moorland vegetation is purposeful: he is straight-lining a course over the contours, only digressing from it when forced to by an inconvenient lump of granite. He is following instinct rather than a path. The breeding season is about to roar into life for him and his kin, and his direction indicates to me that he is making his way towards the dark depths of Sitka spruce that make up the large block of Fernworthy Forest in the heart of the moor, home to a herd of these large mammals.

His size will preclude him from holding the best rutting stands – far larger males will dominate these – but the pheromone-powered draw of the rut is something he cannot ignore. He may have travelled many miles to get here; young male red deer will wander large distances during the rest of the year, leading a sometimes solitary existence, but as autumn gathers pace so too does the urge to return to the herd. He is travelling at a trot, a consistent pace that enables him to cover long distances efficiently. He soon disappears from my sight, slipping over the ridge, continuing his journey across the unnaturally treeless moor, heading for the unnaturally overstocked tree farm beyond.

There are three species of deer that rut in the autumnal months in Britain. The red deer stags famously roar and strut their stuff from here in the South West right across the country to the highlands of Scotland, but the other two species tend to be more overlooked, even though they can be just as noisy. The sika deer is a very close relation to the red deer and indeed interbreeds with it, raising the question of how many of the deer we call red deer are actually hybrids.[71] The sika was introduced to Britain from south-eastern Asia in the Victorian era, and can now be found in scattered populations in many parts of England and Wales, as well as being well established in many parts of Scotland. As closely related as they are, the sika is a very different-sounding animal to the red. Instead of the mighty roar, the sika stags scream a blood-curdling piercing call, a sound that has caused alarm in many a forest walker.

The other autumnal rutter is the widely distributed fallow deer. It can be found across most of England and Wales as well as in scattered locations in southern and central Scotland. It is not native to Britain, being originally from Asiatic Turkey, its range stretching eastwards through the Caucasus region and into Iran. It has been widely introduced by humans and is now present throughout Europe. It was introduced in large numbers in this country by the Normans following the conquest of 1066. It is thought that small numbers were brought over by the Romans too, but whether these survived or not is not known.

The Normans liked to hunt deer within the confines of their new estates and parks, and as in their eyes the fallow deer was a far better choice for this activity than our two natives of red and roe, large numbers of fallow were introduced and released at many sites throughout the country. Deer are very good at getting over and under any fencing or other barriers erected to keep them in, and it wasn't long before wild populations of fallow began to establish. They are now the commonest deer species in England.[72]

I have seen three species of deer around our village in mid-Devon: the odd red feeding in the fields; roe, which are fairly common; and fallow, which although present in good numbers tend to skulk within the cover of woodland – woodland like that which I am in now. The signs that the deer are here are all around me as I walk through the trees: numerous slots[73] dot the bare parts of the ground, and lots of tapered pellets of dung are scattered across the woodland floor, some of them quite fresh. I haven't seen any fallow yet, but I have heard them.

The red's roar is a sound that has often been described as majestic, but the fallow is somewhat less regal in its rutting repertoire. It makes a deep guttural groan, a sound that my daughter once described as sounding like Barney Gumble of *The Simpsons*. As I carefully pick my way between the thin stems of hazel and the larger trunks of oak, detangling my trousers from the snares of bramble, I hear the groaning of a buck[74]

---

71 Guest Blog – 'Just how red are Reds?' by Ian Parsons, published on the markavery.info website 16/11/2017.

72 Data taken from the Mammal Society website: www.mammal.org.uk .

73 The name given to the tracks of deer.

74 The males of Fallow and Roe are called bucks and the females does, whereas the males of Red and Sika are called stags and the females hinds. This is a purely arbitrary labelling.

Unusually in deer, the antlers of the fallow are palmate in form.

resounding through the trees – a large groan followed by shorter bursts of guttural noises – and I can't help but think of my then young daughter's allusion to an indigestion-plagued cartoon character.

I spy a movement through the multitude of stems, a dark subtle motion in amongst the shadows. I realise I am staring at the flank of a fallow. I can only see a small portion of it, but by the size I can tell it is one of this year's young. The melanistic gene, which dominates in the fallow in several parts of Devon, helps the deer to remain unseen in the shadowy depths of the woodland; their coat is not the bright chestnut dappled with white spots that you see in the books, but is a mixture of dark black and grey-brown. Fallow are very variable when it comes to colour, ranging from pure white to black and a whole host of browns in between. The darker coats of the deer here have allowed the youngster in front of me to remain hidden until now.

Another groan reverberates, and this time it is much closer. The young deer is unnerved by it and turns around, walking slowly off in the opposite direction, its ears twitching all the time as it daintily steps through the bramble, avoiding the thorns that never fail to hook into my own legs. More movement of the vegetation, and the buck walks into view; he is a much larger animal than the previous youngster, with a heavy muscular neck that holds his head up high as he smells the air and listens for a response to his calls. He rubs the side of his face against a trunk of a sycamore, daubing it in scent from a gland just below the eye; his antlers give him a clumsy air as he rubs himself on the tree whilst trying to avoid catching the bony growths on it. Satisfied, he turns and looks about him. His antlers are no more than average in size, the flattened palmation of them probably only about 10 centimetres broad. He notices me and stares hard at my form. I feel a thrill of excitement as our eyes lock; at all other times of the year locking eyes with a deer will lead to the deer turning away and removing itself from the scene as quick as it can do, but during the rut testosterone rules the emotions of bucks like this and he doesn't even blink, let alone turn.

We stare at each other through the woodland until he dismisses me as being utterly irrelevant in his pursuit of the does. I am not a challenge to him and therefore I hold no interest, so he breaks the stare, raises his head and sniffs the air before stepping forward once again, following the route he wishes to pursue without once looking back at me. Fallow bucks are big powerful animals, and having a staring contest with one certainly gets the adrenaline flowing.

Arrivals

Halloween, and a cackling chuckle can be heard throughout the countryside – but these are not witches that have descended from high: they are fieldfare. These beautiful thrushes begin to join us in the autumn, their numbers building steadily into the winter months, when well over 700,000 of them can be found across the land,[75] travelling hordes of berry-eaters from the far north of Europe. Strikingly bold birds, their cackling call is

75 BTO BirdFacts, Fieldfare.

the seasonal opposite of the chiffchaff's tuneless tune, bringing with it the shortening days and lengthening nights of autumn and winter.

I hear them for the first time this autumn as I walk along the lanes around the village on a cool grey day, the distinctive call immediately catching my attention, but also initially confusing me as I try to recall its origin. That feeling of knowing you know the call: it's there in your mind, but the name you are seeking seems to evaporate just before you can grasp it. Then, as my memory finally kicks in, so I see them: a loose, scattered flock of about twenty birds, their white under-wings flashing as they flap, the beautiful pale grey of their rump colour matching the sky above them. It is only a brief view, a glimpse of the winter to come, but it is a welcome one. Soon they will be an increasingly common sight, plundering the trees and hedges for the autumnal fruits and staking out the village's many apple trees, enjoying the fallen apples that litter the ground beneath them.

Further on along the lane I see more of them on the ground, a spread-out, busy flock feeding on worms and the like in a damp grassy field. I count forty-six of them, all of them with an air of proudness that their upright posture confers on them as they hop about, moving between the larger, darker rooks that are also feeding in the grassy space. Fieldfares can often be wary birds but in the openness of the hedged-in field they ignore my voyeuristic figure and feed untroubled by my presence. It is great to see them again.

The arrival of the fieldfare is a sure sign of seasonal change.

At the end of the day I take some rubbish out across the patio. It is already dark, and as I head back to the house I hear the other winter thrush flying overhead, the drawn out whistle-like flight call of the redwing a distinctive 'Seep' from the blackness above. The volume of calls suggests that there are lots of birds in the flock, all passing unseen above me in the dark night air.

The nocturnal migration of the redwing is something I always look forward to; like the cackle of the fieldfare, the call of the redwing is yet another of the natural signs that the seasons are again changing. I love standing at the back door on a cold autumnal night, feeling its chill, watching my breath condensing into wispy mists and listening to the flight calls of these beautiful small travelling thrushes. Sometimes they are low enough for me to hear the susurrations of their wings cutting through the darkness, a sound that is even more beautiful than their call.

Both of these winter-visiting thrushes are prodigious travellers: redwings come to us from as far away as Iceland, the very northern edge of Scandinavia, and even the Ural Mountains of central Russia; the majority of the fieldfares, meanwhile, come across the North Sea from Scandinavia, travelling from Finland, Sweden and Norway to take advantage of our relatively mild winters.[76]

The seeps of the redwings grow quieter; the flock has moved past. I have one last look at the black sky above, at the unseen blanket of cloud blocking out the stars, before heading back into the welcoming warmth of the house. It is hard to describe the feeling I

A redwing: listening for their night-time passage is one of my seasonal pleasures.

---

76 Knowledge of our winter thrushes' origins come from ringing recoveries, once again showing the importance of this practice.

Seasonality

get when I first hear the redwings: it is a form of contentment, I guess, a happiness with life. It's strange that an unseen flock of birds can make you feel like that, but that is what these whistling night migrants do to me, year after year. As I settle back into the comforts of the house, my mind is pondering where to look for the new arrivals tomorrow.

Nibbled nuts and whumping badgers

Dazzling diamonds flash from the leaves, captured gems of water from the earlier rain reflecting the low autumn evening sun as I make my way into the wood. There is an abundance of acorns on the woodland floor: ripe, plump, potential progeny of the towering oaks around me. It is undoubtedly a good acorn year, and the woodland's small mammals will be busy storing as many as they possibly can. Fallow deer, which occasionally haunt this wood, will also be taking their share, and the jays will be busy planting them far and wide. Walking between the trees, I cannot help but inadvertently plant some of them myself too, the soles of my feet pushing them down into the soft humus of the woodland floor.

The light has changed since I stepped into the wood; although many of the leaves have already dropped there are still plenty in the canopy above me and the already weak sunlight is diluted further by them. The hazels, remnants of a coppiced past, display their large round leaves at lower levels, sheltered from the leaf-rending winds that rake the upper canopy. Some of the leaves have turned yellow and some have dropped, but the vast majority are still in denial of the seasonal change that is being wrought upon the wood. I walk through the multi-stemmed world of the hazel, pausing to admire the straightness of the stems, occasionally wondering if I need to have another walking stick to whittle and carve.

I tear myself away from coveting the potential sticks and examine the floor beneath them. Here and there lie the broken remains of the tree's eponymous nuts, most neatly cleft in two; they are the work of the grey squirrel, an animal that that has quite an appetite for these nuts. I pick up the two sides of a hatcheted hazelnut, feeling how light they are in my hand. Putting them back together reveals the little notch at the top of the shell where the squirrel has expertly sunk its teeth into the nut to split it cleanly open.

I swipe my foot over the leaf litter at the base of the old coppice stool and reveal a stash of other empty nut cases, but these aren't split open like the others. I know, from the fact that they are in a hidden stash, that they aren't going to be what I am looking for, but I still look, lost in my own little world of being a nature detective. I roll a couple of examples of the evidence around in the palm of my hand, and look at the roundish hole that has been made to extract the nutritious nut from within. The face of the circular cut has obvious little vertical toothmarks all the way around it, and the outside of the nut is scuffed with little marks from the perpetrator's claws. I weigh up the evidence and reach my verdict: a wood mouse has opened these nuts, gathering them one by one, returning to its stash at the base of the tree each time and depositing them one by one, before it has then carefully and meticulously opened each one in turn to feed on the bounty within.

I move my search out a bit further from the coppice stool, away from the mouse's stash, stopping at the point where the branches of the hazel narrow to smaller twigs, a place where the larger, fatter, grey squirrel would struggle to maintain its grip and balance in the flimsy ramified network above. Sure enough, the scatter of neatly split nutshells diminishes greatly, but this far out from the centre of the multi-stemmed tree the light from above penetrates more easily and the floor is more obscured with vegetation. Short, weak stems of bramble and the long, spreading, crawling stems of ivy make it harder to spot the nuts I am looking for, but I soon find one. And then another, and another. These too have a roundish hole in them, but this time the hole is almost perfect in its circularity. There are scuff marks around the cut edge, too, but the cut face is smooth in appearance. No vertical teeth marks are present, just a faint suggestion of some spiralling along it.

These are the smoking gun that this nature detective was seeking, conclusive proof of the common dormouse, a nocturnal and secretive arboreal dweller of woods such as these, a mammal that would be even more under-recorded if it were not for its characteristic manner of opening hazelnuts.[77] Satisfied that I have cracked the case, I move on through the wood, heading for my real objective. I hadn't planned on getting so distracted, but it is so easy to get lost in reverie when examining the secret world that is all around us.

When I get to the battered old oak I have been heading for ever since I left the house, the coming darkness is already thickening the shadows as it creeps into the woods, accompanied by the cold air of the promised clear night to come. The oak is a mess in terms of our normal perception of how a tree should look. Many years ago it suffered a catastrophic failure, its main stem snapping violently about 3 metres up, and the upper part of the tree has long gone – salvaged by firewood seekers perhaps – but the torn stem remained, and sprouted new branches. Three of these arc upwards from the base of the trunk, each one forming a tall sturdy stem that reaches right up into the wood's canopy, but at the point of the break more branches also sprung forth, growing at first laterally before gently inclining upwards. Where they meet the stems growing from the base they form a right-angled mesh of branches, creating a perch in which you can sit and be supported at the same time. It is the perfect spot for what I am wanting to do. You could even say that it is the best seat in the house.

Before me, the wood opens out into a small glade, a hole in the otherwise closed canopy of the wood, the glade is grassy and criss-crossed with small, worn earth paths, it is a busy place, and I only have to wait a couple of minutes to see its first user. A roe buck, freshly shorn of his antlers,[78] enters the stage below me. He picks his way warily along one of the earthen pathways, always listening, always scenting the air. My elevated position puts me out of his eyeline, and my scent doesn't drop to where he is, so I can

---

77 Because the common dormouse opens hazelnuts in such a characteristic manner, the nuts tend to be the way that people survey for this elusive mammal. As a result the dormouse has become heavily linked to hazel, but only in our minds. Common dormice do not need hazel; they will happily exist in areas without this tree.

78 Roe cast their antlers at the beginning of November. The new set will start to become visible in January, as they grow from the skull; while they are growing they are covered in velvet, a thin layer of blood-rich soft skin that will then be frayed off, leaving the bare bone of the antler.

Dormice surely win the prize for being our cutest mammal.

watch him without him realising he is being watched; generally a rare privilege when it comes to watching larger mammals. The deer stops to browse a piece of vegetation, a light piece of munching before he proceeds forwards once more, passing through the glade and vanishing into the increasing murk of the woodland beyond.

The sun has now set, but the glade is still visible, its openness lit by the fading glow of the day just ended. At its far edge I can just make out the outline of the old bank that bisects the woodland, but every minute that passes makes its definition harder to define. I wonder to myself if my late arrival has perhaps disturbed the performers I hoped to see, whether my tangential side-track into the world of the nut-seeking nature detective has inadvertently spoilt my plans. But then I hear them.

The first sound I hear is a dull whump. This is immediately followed by a high-pitched whickering, and then the sound of something running towards the glade. A young badger crashes into my vision, bulldozing through the grasses. A second follows immediately behind it, and as the first one slows, so the second deliberately collides with it and the whump of before is repeated. The two tumble in the glade below me, whickering shrilly as they do so, before abruptly stopping and looking about themselves, almost as if they are surprised to find themselves in the glade.

The light has really faded now, but the black-striped white faces of the badgers below me seem to glow. Our human eyes are not as bad as you might think when it comes to seeing in the dark, especially on clear starry nights like this one. Our problem is that we have become so used to the artificially lit brightness of our existence that our eyes often struggle to adapt when that light is removed. Go out from your back door at night, leave the bright light of the kitchen and enter the unlit garden and you won't see very much at all; but if you wait about twenty minutes, if you allow your eyes to adapt to the low light, you will start to see so much more.

The two youngsters lose interest in their play-fighting and start to snuffle through the grasses and along the bare pathways, I can hear them sniffing and snorting as they go; one of them finds the spot where the roe paused to feed, and it looks up momentarily, smelling the air quizzically, before carrying on its olfactory exploration of the glade. Suddenly a larger badger appears, evidently an adult; it trots its way seriously through the clearing, pausing only to have a scratch at a troublesome itch, raking its right back leg through its fur with vigour. The youngsters watch the bigger animal and then follow on behind it, all three heading off into the trees beyond the glade and beyond my vision. I watch them go, disappointed that they have left so soon, but also pleased that I have shared a few moments with these nocturnal mammals. Shortly after they go, the moon rises, its fullness providing me with some light to aid my descent of the tree, I stand at the bottom of the oak and listen to the movements of the woodland around me: faint rustles of movement in the vegetation, a far-off hoot of a male tawny owl and a brief snatch of whickering badgers, then I turn my attention to picking my way slowly back through the trees.

The moonlight glistens off the tarmac surface of the lane, a silvery film of light broken only by the shadows of trees that form intricate patterns across it. I look through a gateway at the open field beyond: dozens of rabbits are sitting out in the grass, their outlines softened by the light. Five minutes later and I am back in the village, walking down the pavement lit by the overhead street lights that completely drown out the beautiful natural light of the moon; nothing is softened in this light, all outlines are harsh. I follow my sharp-edged shadow homeward.

Autumnal charms

The relentless drizzle continues to fall, dulling the day with its ceaselessness. The weather, though wet, is still very mild – there has been no sign of any autumnal frost – and I sit in the kitchen with the back door wide open, watching the rain against the background of the ivy-clad wall. The dullness of the day is suddenly lifted by the appearance of a small group of goldfinches. I don't see them at first, as they have alighted out of sight in

A goldfinch on one of the feeders in our garden.

the now-bare branches of the hawthorn, but they let me know they are there with their wonderful twinkling, tinkling, trilling, twittering.

I don't move from where I am sitting; I am enjoying listening to their voices and am afraid that if I appear at the door they will take flight. My patience is rewarded when they descend into the lower part of the garden, clearly visible through the back door as they feed in the narrow flower bed that skirts around the front edge of the pond. I am not sure what it is that they are finding as the bed holds a variety of flowering plants that we deliberately allow to go to seed, everything from marjoram to showy cosmos, lungwort and borage, as well as a whole suite of self-seeded garden 'weeds'. Whatever the seeds are that the birds are looking for, it is clear that they are finding them; their bills are busy macerating the seed cases as I watch them from the comfort of my chair.

Goldfinches are such beautiful birds. With a stunning plumage of yellow, black, buff and white, topped off with a wonderful red face mask, they are a bird that is capable of brightening even the dullest drizzle days of autumn, and I can feel my own dull mood lifted by their very presence. They are one of several 'garden' birds that are a British subspecies, differing ever so slightly in plumage and size from the goldfinches on the mainland of Europe.[79]

These are birds that are doing well. Many British birds are undergoing population declines, but the goldfinch is doing the opposite. Its numbers are rising steadily, their population growing and their presence in our gardens, especially in the winter, increasing year on year. Goldfinches feed on small seeds. They used to be able to find these in abundance in our winter farm fields, but as agriculture modernised so the numbers of seeds from so-called agricultural weeds declined. During the 1970s and early 1980s the intensification of agricultural practices was very rapid, and the small seed food sources for many birds simply disappeared. Farmland that was once a fabulous food source turned into a barren desert. Many of Britain's fastest declining small birds belong to a group known as 'farmland' birds, and the goldfinch did indeed suffer, with numbers dropping rapidly during that era. But unlike many of the other 'farmland' birds, the goldfinch has not only stopped the decline but has actually reversed it. It is extremely likely that this increase in numbers has been driven by the bird switching the fields for our gardens and their bird feeders.

It is not clear why the goldfinch has been so easily able to adapt to our bird feeding habits in our gardens when other species of the 'farmland' birds haven't been able to do so, but one thing is clear: the goldfinch is now a very regular garden visitor, even in urban areas. And what a bird to have visiting your garden – they are truly beautiful.

The goldfinches that I can see through the open rectangle of the back door have finished gleaning the soil for seeds. Having sated their appetite they now switch their attention to slaking their thirst, hopping to the edge of the pond and lowering their heads to drink. It is great watching them, especially on such a dull day; they are a charm to watch, just as their group name suggests, but then as they fly off I am reminded of the true meaning of the word 'charm' when it relates to these colourful finches; their individual calls and crystal-clear twitterings blend together to form one sound. In the Oxford English Dictionary there are many definitions of the word 'charm', but in this case the pertinent definition is that of a blend of bird song or bird voices.[80]

The drizzle continues, the day stays dull. But thanks to the visit of the goldfinches I am feeling so much brighter and happier with the day; you could almost say that I have been charmed …

City living

Up above me a peregrine flies, the dark crossbill shape of Baker's prose[81] zipping furiously along, tearing through the sky. I follow it for a few seconds, but it is soon gone, lost in

---

79 Our subspecies is called *Carduelis carduelis britannica* and is found throughout Britain and possibly in the Netherlands as well; it is very slightly smaller and darker than the nominate race found on the mainland continent.

80 First recorded in 1587 as a word relating to the song of birds.

81 *The Peregrine* by J A Baker, first published in 1967, is widely regarded as one of the finest books in the nature writing genre. I have to agree: it is brilliant. If you have never read it, then do so!

the landscape. But it hasn't disappeared behind towering rocky cliffs, nor has it vanished into the background of an estuarine scene as Baker's bird might. No, this peregrine has disappeared behind a multistorey car park. A few seconds later I see it again, this time towering upwards against a background of a vast swath of housing on the city's western flank, and then it is gone again, heading off towards the main train station. This is very much an urban peregrine.

Peregrines are symbols of wildness, of untamed instinct and reckless speeds. We tend to think of their screaming voices as hanging in the wind in untouched landscapes, and whilst these birds can be found in such places they are also commonly found in large cities across the whole of the UK, nesting on the manufactured sheer cliff faces that we call office blocks, cathedrals and churches, and feeding on a wide variety of prey items that pass over and through the urban landscape, as well as predating on those that share the urban spaces with it.

There is always something exhilarating about seeing a peregrine, watching the fastest of the fast; there is something special about seeing them in a wild landscape, but there is also something special about seeing them in the human-dominated urban worlds we have created. They are a connection, a connection away from the bricks and the mortar, the concrete and the steel, the tarmac and the vehicles, a connection to the natural world, a connection that we desperately need. Our urban environments are far removed from anything we could call natural, but if you are able to look up and see this avian apex predator flashing across the skyline then not only does it bring exhilaration, it also brings hope. And even a sort of reassurance that nature is never that far away.

I turn the corner and enter the busy High Street, immediately having to shorten my step to avoid a pigeon that is intent on finishing off some human-dropped morsel of food. The nest ledges of our urban cliffs are an attraction for the falcon, but so are these plump, numerous and somewhat laid-back descendants of the peregrine's natural prey, the rock dove. These feral birds have had their flight-or-fight edge eroded away by domestication and urban living, they haven't been exposed to the constant threat of predators and they have been living on Easy Street – but now in virtually all of the large cities across Britain they are having their survival wits sharpened by the presence of a predator. And not just any predator: the peregrine, the perennial pigeon pursuer.

The street is busy with people. The shops are, as is the norm for autumn, prematurely bedecked with Christmas items, and everywhere is hustle and bustle. It is not an environment that I feel comfortable in, but I do take comfort from the fact that somewhere high above me a peregrine falcon is likely to be sitting on a concrete ledge, watching the river-like flow of people below it with an uninterested air.

We almost wiped out the peregrine. Our love of introducing created chemicals into agriculture in the 1950s and 1960s almost sounded the death knell for this and many other rapacious species, the lethal toxins concentrating their way up through the food chain and reaching lethal levels. Eventually the worst chemicals were banned, and slowly but surely these fast falcons have regained lost ground, rediscovering natural nest sites on cliffs and rocky ridges and discovering a whole host of new ones on our built infrastructure of pylons, industrial chimneys and buildings of all descriptions. They are back and doing. There are now around 1750 pairs,[82] but they are still persecuted by a selfish few who seek to destroy our natural treasures, who seek to deprive the vast majority of people in this country the opportunity and the pleasure of seeing the exhilaration of a peregrine in flight.

Autumnal arachnids and colonising bees

Autumn is the season for seeing spiders. Our herb bed outside the back door is festooned with the beautiful classic webs of the garden spider, the maker of each web smack bang in the centre of its ornate but deadly snare. These are beautiful spiders, with a cross-like pattern on their abdomens, and they are also one of our commonest species, one we can all enjoy. The ones in our herb bed, like the ones in the rest of the garden, have spent the night constructing their orb web so that it is now ready for the daily passage of small flying insects. The trap is set. The autumn is the best time to see these harmless (to humans at least) and beautiful arachnids: they seem abundant and at their prime, but in reality this is their swansong.

There is one web right outside the door: it is evidently well placed as there are numerous parcels of food, wrapped up tightly in silk, dotted across its sticky threads. The spider in this web is the much larger female; she will have mated with a smaller male back in the summer, and it is likely that she will have then eaten him. After all, a nice nutritious source of protein is just what the developing eggs within her will have needed.

Her eggs will be laid in a soft silken cocoon, a precious parcel that she will protect diligently until the first frosts of the year arrive. It is these frosts that will most likely kill her. Her time is coming to an end, but the eggs will survive the meteorological shock, remaining dormant in their carefully wrapped parcel until next spring, when they will hatch out into a myriad of spiderlings that will cluster together in little balls for security, exploding outward in all directions if disturbed.

There is no shortage of spiders indoors at this time of year, either; male house spiders are regularly found wandering across a floor in the morning in their search for a female to mate with, and occasionally one falls into the giant pitfall trap that we humans call a bath, floundering along on the long legs that can find no purchase on its slithery vertical sides.[83] In the corners of the rooms there lurks another long-legged species, its limbs so long in comparison to its body that it has earned the species the sobriquet of the daddy long-legs spider. They may look feeble on their seemingly impossibly thin legs, but they are extremely predacious, hunting all manner of invertebrates including other spiders, many of which are bigger than they are. If we inadvertently disturb them in their webs

---

82 BTO BirdFacts, Peregrine.

83 Despite many people believing that the spiders they find in the bath have come up through the plughole, they will have all fallen in from above, because even if any have explored up inside the drainpipe, the water in the u-bend will have defeated them.

they use their long legs to cause a strong vibration through the silken mesh, and this throws them into a high-speed circular motion as they ride the violently moving strands of silk. It has to be said that this defence is not very effective against a feather duster or a vacuum cleaner, but then they didn't evolve it to battle such modern-day predators. However, for defending themselves against attack from other spiders or even their own kind – they will readily resort to cannibalism – it is highly effective, as the rapidly moving blur in the web is very difficult for the aggressor to target with any accuracy.

These eight-legged predators are largely disliked by the majority of us humans. Indeed many of us have a phobia of them, a fear learnt from our parents when we were small children, their reactions to these tiny small invertebrates imprinted deep in our brains. For many this fear is based on fangs, despite the fact that the vast majority of spiders in Britain have fangs so tiny that even if they wanted to bite us (and why would they?) they would be unable to do so. However, one spider that does have fangs large enough to bite us is commonly found around the outside of our houses – but before you start to conjure up images of giant tropical-looking tarantulas, let me point out that not only will it not bite you unless you actively make it, but also that its bite, whilst painful, is harmless.

The woodlouse spider is well named, for it does indeed feed on woodlice, but it also feeds on centipedes, millipedes, earwigs, beetles and other spiders. It is a top predator of the invertebrate world, a supreme hunter, and it will take anything it can catch. They may be top predators, but they are diminutive in size, generally measuring just over one

Autumn

centimetre in length. For their small size, however, they have huge fangs and can look quite fearsome if looked at closely. It is these fangs that are used to capture their prey, piercing the tough, plated carapace of woodlice and the like. Their fangs are armour-piercing weapons.

But aside from their close-up fearsome looks, they are actually attractive creatures; with a red carapace and a grey/pink abdomen, they are far more worthy of admiration than fear. We have one that lives under a plant pot on our kitchen windowsill, spending the day in a silken tent that it has woven in a crevice in the render. Even though these spiders will weave themselves a tent in which to shelter, they aren't web spinners. Their method of hunting is different to the web spinners we are all familiar with; instead of setting silken snares and waiting for their prey to come to them, they go out looking for their prey, actively stalking about after dark; they are invertebrate night prowlers, exploring damp places and the like in their search for prey to snatch. They are very common, and you are likely to have them very near to wherever you are reading this. Basically, if you have woodlice then you are very likely to have their eponymous predator as well. But that is no need to feel threatened; just because they are one of the very few

A woodlouse spider in the safe confines of a glass after being found wandering across our lounge floor.

British spiders able to bite us doesn't make them aggressive. In fact they are the complete opposite; if you uncover one while moving a flower pot or doing some gardening, they will run away, actively seeking dark sanctuary once again, and it is only if you decide to handle them roughly that they are likely to bite you. Admire their beauty without picking them up, and you won't get bitten. Simple.

The ivy on the wall in our garden, the ivy on the trees in the landscape around the village, and the ivy that bedecks some old outbuildings along one of our favourite walks is all in flower now. We think of spring as being the time for wild flowers, but ivy bucks that trend: its flowers start to appear in late summer and carry on through to late autumn. They are rich in nectar and a vital food source for many invertebrates, including many butterflies that hibernate as adults.[84] These beautiful insects are able to feed up on the ivy's sugary fuel and lay down much-needed resources before they enter into their winter sleep. But it is not just these late-flying butterflies that exploit this nectar resource. Autumn is the time to see one of our more unusual bee species, a recent arrival to our shores. The ivy bee is a bee that revolves its life around the flowers of the plant with which it shares its name.

The ivy bee was first found in mainland Britain in the county of Dorset in 2001,[85] and since then it has spread across the southern half of Britain, the entire south coast of the country now colonised and with records of it as far apart as north Norfolk and Pembrokeshire.[86] They are the last of our solitary bees to emerge as adults, with males appearing first at the beginning of September and then the females a couple of weeks later. If the autumn weather stays frost-free, which it generally does in Devon, they can still be on the wing in November. If you see a bee buzzing around ivy in the autumn you are likely to be looking at an ivy bee.

Their requirements are simple: ivy. The flowers of this evergreen woody climber are the bee's food source, which is why their emergence is so late in the season, coinciding with the appearance of the nectar-laden flowers. Although they are solitary bees, they can actually form large nesting colonies, making their individual nesting chambers in the soil of sparsely vegetated areas, especially those with a sunny aspect. Coastal cliffs and heathlands are used, but so are lawns, allotments and parks, bringing this late-flying bee right into the areas where we live.

They belong to a group known as plasterer bees, a group so named because the bees line or, if you prefer, plaster their nest tunnels with a substance produced in their mouths that helps to waterproof the tunnel and is also believed to have anti-fungal properties.[87]

---

84 A number of British butterflies do this, including the red admiral and the peacock.
85 *Field Guide to the Bees of Great Britain and Ireland*, Falk, Bloomsbury, 2015.
86 Data taken from the website of the Bees, Wasps and Ants Recording Society: www.bwars.com .
87 *Field Guide to the Bees of Great Britain and Ireland*, Falk, Bloomsbury, 2015.

Most plasterer bees have a distinctive banded abdomen, and the ivy bee is a good example of this, having very noticeable broad orangey bands around its otherwise dark abdomen.

If you are really lucky you may see a phenomenon known as a mating ball: as the females start to emerge from their burrow, the males seize their opportunity, and when several males try to mate with the one female the males can end up entangled with one another as they grapple to secure mating rights. In larger colonies these grapples can involve dozens of males, and it is an impressive site to see a ball of angry males scrapping on the ground. Underneath them, though, is the female, who is probably less than impressed!

On a sunny autumn day, the ivy flowers are busy places, literally abuzz with flying insects. There are many wasps feeding on the sweet nectar, and a wide variety of small fly species, but it doesn't take me long to spot first one, then two, then three ivy bees, their broad bands on their rear ends really standing out as they crawl over the clusters of small flowers that the ivy produces. The insects get the nectar as a reward, and while the ivy bees are enjoying this, they are also collecting pollen to take back to their newly dug nesting chambers, where it will be laid down as a provision for the next generation of this beautiful little bee. The ivy of course benefits from all this activity by having its flowers pollinated; they will shortly set seed and form the ivy berries so favoured by the blackbirds and thrushes that will visit them later this autumn and into the winter.

Ivy berries are a vitally important food source for many birds.

These birds are the ivy's main propagators, depositing the seeds in new locations. The ivy produces the flowers, the insects feed on these and pollinate them, and then the birds feed on the resulting berries, sustaining themselves whilst also planting the next generation of ivy that will soon be ready to produce flowers for the future generations of insects like the ivy bee that feed on the flowers and pollinate them … And so it goes on – but only if, in the human-dominated world in which we live, we allow it to.

Humans always seem to be waging a war against ivy: many of us see it as a pest, something that we should eradicate or at the very least control. But the simple truth is that ivy is one of the most important plants in Britain for wildlife, providing cover, nest sites, hibernation sites and a whole gamut of feeding opportunities throughout the year. But ivy is good for us too: it is a great trapper of atmospheric dust, and it can provide us with great nature that we can enjoy right outside our homes. Perhaps unexpectedly, it can also save us money and help us to reduce our vast energy consumption. Ivy is conventionally seen as a threat to our houses in that we believe that it damages walls, but the simple truth is that the aerial roots of ivy cannot penetrate sound, well-maintained walls. If our houses are looked after, then ivy on the walls is not a threat; indeed recent scientific papers have shown that it is a tremendous benefit.[88] Ivy-clad walls of a house cool its internal temperature in the summer months, reducing the need for air conditioning, and then in the winter the ivy acts as an insulator, helping to reduce heat loss through the external walls of the building, trapping warmth inside the property and reducing its heating requirements. It helps with humidity too, lowering the relative humidity inside the property. In short, ivy is great.

Autumn whites

White gulls are dotted all across the red-brown soils of the morning's freshly ploughed fields; these newly worked areas are now liberally adorned with the shiny white plumage of these supposed seagulls. The birds form random patterns, modern works of art to be viewed from above, their gleaming plumage sharply contrasting against the darker rich colours of Devon's famous red earth. A decoration of gulls would be a good collective noun for such gatherings, but the birds are not here to decorate; they are here to harvest the collateral of the plough, to pick up and feast upon the broken. They are the opportunists of the bird world, and this morning's ploughing has given them the opportunity of a feast that they are not refusing.

I watch the birds for several minutes through my binoculars, enjoying the brightness of the gulls and the colours in the soil, both of which are highlighted by the strong sunlight. The birds are a mixture of both herring and lesser black-backed gulls, two birds that started off as one bird before spreading out around the globe and meeting back up again as two separate species. Gull identification can be a bit complex, and indeed the two species I am watching form something known as the herring gull/lesser black-backed gull complex. In simple terms, the complex has a distribution that circles the

88 *Cool Climbers*, RHS Members' magazine, February 2021.

globe, ringing the northern hemisphere. In doing so the birds have evolved into adjacent populations and although these are closely related, they are slightly different from their immediate neighbours. It just so happens that each end of this global distribution meets up here, and that the birds at each end of this very complex complex are the herring gull and the lesser black-backed gull. By now, the slight differences have accumulated, and the two birds are easily recognised as being separate species even though they are very closely related – so closely, in fact, that they can interbreed, although this doesn't happen as often as it could considering that they coexist alongside one another.

Moving on along the footpath, trying to avoid getting bogged down in the complexities of complexes, as well as the muddy mess that is the path's surface, I leave the white gulls to their scavenging and go looking for more eye-catching whiteness. I am heading for a couple of fields over, a field that is a bit of a rarity these days in our intensively farmed landscape. It is a scruffy and unkempt field. It is a bit of a graveyard for old farm equipment: a couple of tractors are quietly rusting away in it, and there are numerous other weird and wonderful-looking pieces of old chunky metal devices scattered about the place. A large pile of manure rots in the centre of the field, and a couple of old circular bales of straw are busy decomposing in an ungainly heap. The metal debris precludes any cutting regime and any grazing by clumsy livestock; instead the grass has been let go and is a mosaic of tussocky clumps. The hedge nearest the tractors has escaped the flail, and as a result the bramble and the blackthorn have tumbled out of the confines of the stock fence and are busy advancing into the grassland. One of the tractors has already been reached, and last summer's bramble runners are grasping at its front axle.

I wonder how many walkers along this public footpath bemoan the untidiness of it, but the untidiness of it is brilliant for wildlife. Unlike the sterile but neat fields I have been walking through, this scruffy mess of a field is full of birds. There are a couple of pied wagtails wagging their tails around the sprawling dung heap, numerous starlings feeding in amongst the fallen-over grasses, several blackbirds and at least one song thrush in the spreading hedge, and a group of goldfinch feeding on a clump of thistles that have grown up through a tangle of old metal angle-iron posts. But it is the mass of birds feeding on the ground around the collapsed and degrading old bales that has drawn me here. The old straw in the bales has been pulled apart and scattered over a large area of the field that slopes away from where I am standing on the muddy path, and in amongst the straw are lots and lots of small birds feeding on the seeds within the strewn contents of the huge old bales. It is here that I look for whiteness.

There are several house sparrows, but the majority of the birds are finches. Chaffinches predominate, but there is also a handful of bramblings, and it is these that I am after. Bramblings are very closely related to chaffinches, and when they join us in the autumn and winter months[89] their plumage is similar enough for you to need to have to have a close look at the birds as they feed all together on the ground. Although looking for

---

89 Arriving on our shores from mid-September and staying until the end of March (sometimes later), their numbers can vary dramatically year on year depending on food availability on the continental mainland. Some years we can have only a few tens of thousands of them; in other years their numbers can approach two million.

white, I am also looking for a colour that is uncommon in British birds: orange. I soon spot some, the males first. With their more lavish splash of orange on their breasts and darker head these male bramblings stand out more from the chaffinches than do the females, which have a more subtle daub of orange and a head pattern that closely resembles the females of their relation.

There are several of them on the ground, scattered among the other birds that are all feeding away; occasionally one turns so that its back is facing me and then I can see the telltale white of the rump peeking through between the folded wings. This is the white I have been seeking. The big difference in the plumages of the chaffinch and the brambling is this white rump of the latter; if something spooks these birds in front of me, the flash of white as the birds fly away is immediately obvious. It is a seasonal semaphore, signalling to anybody watching that autumn has arrived and with it so have the bramblings. They have travelled from their breeding grounds in Scandinavia and northern Russia; they have undertaken a migration to escape the frozen climes there, coming here to feed on our seeds, seeds that won't be trapped beneath a thick layer of frozen snow.

I watch the large feeding flock for some time, watch its movements and its undulations as the birds move *en masse* across the surface of the ground. There are some linnets and goldfinches in amongst the birds, helping to create a pretty patterned carpet of feathery delight. As I head for home, another white-rumped finch catches my eye, bouncing along the hedge line in front of me before perching up on a dead bramble stem. It is a bullfinch, a male judging by the intensity of its colouration: another beauty of a bird for me to enjoy.

Garden visits

The autumnal shower is replaced by some autumnal sun. I look out of the bedroom window at the garden beyond, the leaves of the smoke bush in the foreground a mixture of yellows and greens. Everything looks tired now, and the leaves of the hawthorn have lost their vibrancy, especially when compared to the bright red berries that hang like decorations all over the tree. A wood pigeon is sitting on top of the largest cloche. I look at it as I sit down on the window seat and it doesn't react to my presence at all; instead, it is absolutely stock still, rigid in its pose. I wonder why it is acting like it is, wonder why it isn't shuffling about or looking around as the pigeons that visit the garden normally do – and then I see a shape behind it, a shape nestled tight into the trunk of the goat willow pollard that I will soon be cutting back once the remaining leaves that hang tattily from its branches have dropped.

The brown shape is a tawny owl, and it is staring straight at me as I sit staring back from the bedroom. The poor pigeon is sitting right in the middle and probably feels that it is the subject of the stares. Caught in the view of two predators it just stays there unmoving, clearly unsure of what to do. The owl is beautiful in its repose, a delight to see in daylight rather than the dark shadowy shape of the night that I normally see; the lighter markings on its plumage look exactly like dappled sunlight on the bark of the

As I looked through the window I noticed a woodpigeon acting strangely, and then I noticed a dark shape in the goat willow beyond …

Seasonality

… a tawny owl!

tree, a perfect demonstration of the bird's cryptic colouration. The owl loses interest in me and swivels its head around, turning those dark impenetrable pools of eyes away from my own as it looks about itself.

For a daytime roost for these night-time birds the willow seems somewhat exposed, and I wonder if the owl has been disturbed from a more suitable site. I haven't seen it there before, although I have noticed white splattered droppings on the garden below the tree in the past, indicative of an owl or raptor. The predatory bird seems untroubled by my watching of it; it looks back at me a couple of times, but does so in an uninterested way, preferring to look over the wall and into the large laurels beyond the boundary, and I wonder if this would be its normal roost; the tall unruly evergreen member of the cherry family would certainly provide it with plenty of cover, keeping it hidden from the small birds who are always ready to noisily mob a tawny should they find one in the daytime.

After several minutes, the wood pigeon that has remained motionless on the cloche opts to make a move, and with the owl looking the other way it suddenly takes to the wing in its usual clattering fashion. The noise and commotion of the bird taking off causes the tawny to swivel its head back around, but not in a manner that displays any predatory interest. It does, however, seem a little more alert, standing higher on its legs, looking taller on the perch; as I watch the bird it lifts its short tail, leans forward and shoots a white stream of poo onto the garden below, then gives itself a good shake-down before it drops off the perch, opening its long wings and swiftly banking around before heading off into the depths of next door's laurels.

I leave my vantage point and head outdoors into the garden. At the base of the willow is the telltale white splat of the owl, gleaming white against the darkening fern leaves that it has partially covered. Looking closer I can see that there are the older, dryer and duller remains of further white splat, telling me that this perch is most definitely not a new one for the owl. I have a bit of a scratch about in the leaf litter and under the fern to see if I can find a pellet, the regurgitated remains of the owl's diet, but sadly I can't locate one. Instead I head back inside and grab one of my trail cameras; it is going to tell me if the owl returns to the goat willow at night.

The following morning, before I even make the coffee, I am clicking through the recordings on the trail camera – and there, to my utmost delight, is the tawny owl, perched on the same branch as it was during the day, filling the screen with its infrared-lit presence, looking around itself and studying the ground below. It's not much, but the thrill of knowing that the tawny owl is using our goat willow in our garden certainly makes the coffee taste even better this morning.

It is a constant motion, a continuous movement, hanging off the tips of the hawthorn, dropping on to the trunk, then moving instantly to the ivy. It is so busy, so frenetic, that it is virtually impossible to get a good look at it, but the flash of colour on top of its head, even though it is really just a small blur within a slightly larger blur, is all I need to see to know that a goldcrest is in the garden. These are our smallest birds, even smaller than the more familiar and much commoner wren.[90] The goldcrest is a woodland insect feeder that is pushed into the gardens of the village at this time of year in its endless search for enough food to keep it going.

Goldcrests are resident birds in Britain, but on the east coast of the country those residents are joined by others migrating to our shores for the winter months from Scandinavia. It is incredible when you think about it: these tiny birds, weighing less than a 2p coin,[91] fly straight across the North Sea. The North Sea is famed for being rough, but even if it was a flat calm sea of tranquillity this distance over water should still be a monumental challenge. The fact that it is apparently not, and the fact that a goldcrest is just one gram heavier than a sheet of A4 copier paper, makes the bird completely remarkable, to my mind. Folklore tells a brilliant story to explain how these tiny birds make such an epic journey: they apparently catch a lift off the woodcock, riding on its back across the waves. If only it was true. We are not the only country that these tiny birds migrate to: ringing data has shown that goldcrests also migrate from Finland to the Spanish Balearics – a ridiculous straight-line distance of over 1,600 miles.

Every year we get goldcrest in the garden. Here in the South West of Britain they will be local birds as opposed to Scandinavian ones, moving from the nearby countryside into the village and its gardens, usually accompanying foraging flocks of tits. Not for them the winter sun of Mallorca. But we only get these great little birds now, as the temperature starts to drop and the day length really dwindles down. For us, these tiny feathered balls are a wintering garden bird, and their arrival in the hawthorn is as sure a sign that winter is arriving as anything on a calendar.

90 Wrens measure 10 cm in length, have a wingspan of 15 cm and weigh 10 g: Goldcrests measure 9 cm in length, have a wingspan of 14 cm and weigh just 6 g.
91 A 2p coin weighs 7.12 g.

Winter

Winter rushes in with a depressive weather system of strong winds and persistent rains. Gales rake the trees, relieving them of the remainder of their leaves, creating swirling clouds of redundant foliage before they are beaten down and flattened by the heavy rain. With the low pressure comes a notable lowering of the air temperature, and a mass of blackbirds appear, squabbling over the red fruits of the hawthorn, eating copious amounts, denuding the tree of its produce as the wind strips the last of its leaves. Our white-dotted male is there, but the youngster that was a regular in our kitchen isn't. Just as the autumn came to an end he vanished – I say 'he' because in the last few days that the bird was in the garden it had started to very quietly, very discreetly, sing. It didn't open its bill when doing so, it wasn't full-on song; it was as if the bird had found its voice and was quietly exploring it. It is typical behaviour of a young juvenile male, but it is behaviour that brings it into potential conflict with other males, perhaps even his white-dotted father. We don't know what happened to him; we can only hope that he is exploiting a food source elsewhere, but the reality for young birds is that life is difficult; only about half of young fledged blackbirds make it to the next calendar year.

I have some hope: the several blackbirds that are in the hawthorn are all adults, so perhaps he has joined a group of youngsters that are now choosing to feed away from the more dominant birds. One thing is for certain, though: blackbirds like hawthorn berries, and I happily watch them gulping down the tree's offering before coughing up the large seed within. Most of them seem to fall onto the patio, but we know from experience that many fall on to the beds and into the pots; we will never be short of seedling hawthorns in our garden.

We don't tend to think of blackbirds as being migrants – indeed our population is largely termed resident – but even so, many of our birds still make winter movements. These are often quite short, the birds exploiting an abundance of food near where they were feeding in the summer and autumn, but other birds can travel long distances within Britain. One ringed bird famously travels from a garden in Norfolk to a garden in Devon every winter,[92] but others travel further still, with one bird ringed on the first of April in 2014 at Fair Isle, in the Shetland Islands, turning up in a ringer's net in November of that year at the completely opposite end of Britain, on the Isle of Portland,[93] the large outcrop of limestone that juts out into the Channel from the coast of Dorset. The trapping location suggests very strongly that this was a blackbird that was heading to the Continent for the winter months.

But just as some of our birds head to continental Europe for the winter, so do other birds from the north of the Continent head to us. The blackbirds of Scandinavia are highly migratory, and some of these head across the North Sea to our shores whilst others head south-west to spend the winter in the Iberian peninsula. All this is known only because of the ringing data, showing how important this simple practice is in understanding the behaviour of birds.

We of course see blackbirds all the time; they are ever present in our gardens, and it is very easy to assume that the birds we are seeing are the same individuals week after week, month after month, throughout the year. We are lucky that 'our' male has leucistic markings making him an individual we can recognise, but this winter we have a large number of other blackbirds feeding on the hawthorn in our garden and on the holly in next door's. Are they birds that spend the whole year in the village or, as is likely, are some of them from further afield, be that elsewhere in Britain or even in Scandinavia? I always think that one of the great things about watching wildlife is the pondering on questions about what you are seeing, attempting to explain the events that unfold before you; often, though, the interpretation of the facts leads to yet more questions. As we watch the blackbirds in our garden at the beginning of this new season, those questions revolve around just one bird. Is the young male still alive? Is he in the village, or is he perhaps flicking through the leaves in an olive grove somewhere in the south of Spain?

Substitute pigs and nervy voles

A dark morning, the new day no more than an inchoate glimmer on the eastern horizon. The density of the darkness seems to smother all beyond the cone of light cast from the open kitchen door. But then that dense blackness is cleaved by the clear, clean, razor sharpness of a robin's elegiac song, welcoming the new day before it has even dawned. I treat the song like a summons to action, and duly oblige in my duty, scattering a handful of mealworms across the patio before placing a few more on the post that supports the steps, a post that is illuminated by the light emanating from the kitchen window.

I retreat back into the electric dazzle of the house, starting the morning coffee ritual whilst keeping one eye on the post outside. I don't have to wait long. The robin has stopped its musical interlude and now appears on the post facing me in the illuminated kitchen; it tilts its head at me before greedily devouring the mealworms, scattering their crumbs in all directions. I have been well trained: the bird sings and I respond. Stimulus, response.

92 BTO BirdFacts, Blackbird.
93 BTO ringing data.

There are many of us that have a robin in our lives, but if you haven't, allow yourself to be trained by one. The reward is an indescribable joy. The gardener's friend, our Robin Redbreast, accompanies us as we dig over the soils, weed the beds, rake the leaves and move the pots. Everyone loves a robin, a bird that seems to seek us out, that seems to enjoy our companionship. A bird full of anthropomorphic character, a bird that brings colour and song to gloomy winter days, a bird that symbolises the 'Season's Greetings' adorning millions of Christmas cards, a bird that murders its own kind,[94] a bird that thinks we are no more than a pig.

The spectacles that we view the robin through are so rose-tinted that they have thorns. This isn't a bird that sings for us to bring cheer to the winter gloom, this isn't a bird that accompanies us to lift our spirits, this isn't a bird that wants to be our friend. This is a bird, a bird like every other bird, engaged in the constant struggle for survival. It is thought that the robin evolved in the woodlands that would once have dominated the European continent. But those woods were not the closed canopy systems we often imagine them to be; they would have been dynamic habitats, managed by nature, an ever-varying mosaic of open ground, scrubby ground and wooded ground, constantly changing and constantly shaped by the species that lived within them.

---

94 In some areas up to 10 per cent of adult mortality is caused by other robins fighting over territory.

Winter

One of those species would have been the wild boar, a porcine digging machine constantly rooting through the soils, grubbing up the ground, unearthing the earth, creating wallows of open mud. To some humans this behaviour is seen as destructive, but in actual fact it is the complete opposite. It is creative. Wild boar are habitat creators: they create disturbed ground; they create bare ground that colonising plants require, bare ground that many insects and other invertebrates depend upon. So their activities lead to diversity – and also lead to feeding opportunities for birds like the robin. Furrowing their plough-like heads through the leaf litter and the soil of a woodland, these wild pigs disturb and expose a whole assortment of invertebrates. The robin has always lived alongside the boar, and for thousands and thousands of years the bird would have followed any boars moving through its territory, carefully watching the animal's activity and always alert to any opportunity that arose from it, swooping down to snaffle any worm or grub that these dark hairy pigs uncovered. To the robin, the wild boars were a mechanism that created feeding opportunities; they were a large mammal that it was profitable for the small bird to hang around by.

We extirpated wild boar from our country sometime between the 11th and 15th centuries. Charles I tried to reintroduce them into the New Forest in the 17th century, but the Civil War put paid to that, and to him. Without the pig they had evolved with, robins would have turned to that other great disturber of soils, us. When we are digging the vegetable bed over, when we are weeding the flower beds, when we are raking up

How the robin sees us? A wild boar disturbing the
ground and producing potential robin food.

leaves or rearranging the pots, we are in the eyes of the robin mimicking the rooting and snuffling behaviour of the wild boar; we are just another large mammal exposing invertebrates and creating feeding opportunities for the red-breasted bird that we like to think of as a friend.

But does that really matter? Does it matter that the robin is simply following innate behaviour when it trails us closely when we are in the garden working? Of course it doesn't; we are getting a connection through the interaction, a connection that makes us feel good, a connection that releases endorphins into our neurological system. The robin might look on us as a sort of large bipedal pig, but we think they're brilliant and they make us happy – and that, at the end of the day, is what counts.

It doesn't see me watching it. I'm looking out of the upstairs window, looking down onto the patio and the scattering of mealworms upon it. A bank vole has appeared, a small brown bundle of nervous energy. It can smell the mealworms just a short distance away, tempting it out onto the bare open plain of the patio. It makes short, hesitant bursts from plant pot to plant pot, trying to get as close to the food as it can without exposing itself to danger, then a quick foray out onto the coverless concrete, snatching a mealworm before a blurred dash back to the sanctuary of cover under the steps.

A few seconds later it appears again, edging out from the under-step darkness, I get a good look at its face through my binoculars: the eyes blank but not quite, filled with curious incuriosity as it sits there, nose twitching, smelling the reward of risk. Its ears are partially hidden within the fur. This lack of prominent ears distinguishes it easily from the wood mice that also inhabit the garden, while the reddish-brown fur, combined with the proportionally long tail, distinguish it from the very similar and closely related field vole. Then it is off again: a brief dash to the first pot, pause, sniff, then off to the next, before sprinting out towards the mealworms, snatching one up and turning all in one movement, and heading back to cover. The highly strung small mammal does this four more times, but then on its fifth attempt it unwittingly coincides its outward sprint with the attempted landing of a female blackbird. The dark shape of a rapidly descending bird just above its head is too much for the vole, and it instantly forgets the mealworm and turns tail, dashing back in under the steps. The blackbird too is unnerved by the previously unseen rodent and its lightning-quick movement, so instead of landing she arcs upwards and away, alarm-calling loudly. I take pity on the bank vole and head outside with a few mealworms which I place well into the shadow of the steps, an offering that will hopefully help its blood pressure.

Voles are very common animals in Britain: the two main species, bank and field, probably have a combined population of around 100 million individuals.[95] They are right to be of a nervous disposition, for they are the mainstay of many predator diets, be they

95 Data taken from the website of the People's Trust for Endangered Species, www.ptes.org .

The bank vole crossing the openness of the patio to get to the mealworms.

avian, mammalian or even reptilian. It could therefore be argued that voles are the most important mammals in Britain. They are active throughout the year, but now is the time that they seem to be more visible, visiting the ground beneath bird feeders, scrounging for scraps to help them through the colder days and nights. A careful look along a hedge bank will show their runs and burrows, exposed by the winter regress of vegetation. They can be found pretty much everywhere; they even use our thatch, their nocturnal scurryings testament to their presence above us.

They are often habitual in their usage of their runs and pathways, a habit that some predators exploit, concentrating their hunting efforts in well-used areas.[96] The bank vole that I have been watching snatching mealworms from the patio will have used the busy vole highway that takes it from next door's garden into ours, a highway that then carries on underneath the top step of the wooden stairs that connect our lower garden to the upper part. This well-used route then proceeds through the cover of the fern and St John's wort, but then the cover vanishes and the traveller has to make a quick dash across the exposed top of the stone wall before plunging into the deep cover of the sprawling ivy. At this point the main highway splits into a myriad of different routes, allowing the vole traffic to access all parts of the garden.

From here, if the vole is heading for the mealworms on the patio, its progress can be

96 A good example is the common kestrel. The hovering bird that you see over the grassy embankment hasn't just randomly chosen this spot to hang in the air over; it has chosen it because the area below is probably an interchange of small mammal runs, a busy vole junction and therefore a profitable place to hunt.

followed by the telltale twitching of the ivy leaves growing on the vertical wall, before the small mammal appears as a brown blur for the last few inches, running vertically down the bare stone and vanishing into the unkempt vegetation around the back of the pond. Again, vegetative twitching maps the progress of the small mammal before it will inevitably appear on the mossy stones behind the apple tree, housed in its large raised metallic tub. A quick drop down to the floor sees the vole then sprint under this tub, from whence it peers out, cautiously examining the scene, before stealthily making its way along the bottom of the flowerbed-retaining wall, taking advantage of the cover provided by the curtain of periwinkle leaves that hang down it. The vole then, finally, gets to the security of the pots by the bottom of the steps. It is a circuitous route, to say the least, but the lure of the mealworm is strong.

Avian social networking

Another wet, cold morning slowly, reluctantly, dawns. The darkness gradually dilutes, becoming increasingly watered down as the eastern sky burns brighter by the minute, and as it does so dark shapes are revealed in the skeletal beech trees that line the road around the large secondary school in our nearest town. Christmas is coming, the festive time of year when we adorn trees with decorations, harking back to pagan celebrations of the past. But these tree-borne decorations are not symbols of our offerings to imagined gods; they are entirely natural, they are corvid in origin. A conglomeration of rooks and jackdaws fill the trees with their blackness: shadows of restless, noisy energy in the watery light. Stopped at the traffic lights, you can hear them even through the glass windows of the car, hear their calls over the throb of engines, the harsh 'Tchak' of the jackdaws and the more sonorous 'Graaah' of the rooks. Morning chatter before work begins.

The lights turn to green and the traffic flows forth, humans in regular lines and corvids in irregular flocks. But the mixed flocks of jackdaws and rooks leaving the relative warmth of the town aren't irregular in their movements. Like the people in the morning traffic below them, they know exactly where they are headed. To us, these departing corvids may appear noisy and chaotic, but perhaps that is a reflection of what the birds see when they watch us on our own morning peregrinations.

Mid-winter corvid gatherings are fascinating to watch, accessible animal behaviour often happening right outside our houses as the birds take advantage of our heating of our environment. It may feel cold to us when we step outside of our homes in cities, towns and villages during this darkest month, but it will be warmer than the surrounding countryside. It may be only by a degree or two, but these small differences can be vital for wildlife struggling to survive a long cold night.

But the birds don't just get warmth from these gatherings; they also get social contact and information. Both the rook and the jackdaw are highly social animals; they like the company of others. But they also form a stable monogamous breeding pair for life, remaining in their pair even in the large winter flocks. These pairs form extended social groups and exchange information, a social media of loud and raucous twittering.

The rook is a beautiful and highly social bird.

Information on food sources is passed on; exactly how is not fully understood, but it has been shown that birds that have discovered an abundance of food one day will return to it the next with birds that weren't there previously. File sharing in social networks is not just a human thing.

By the time I get to the other end of the High Street, the clouds of corvids above have dissipated; they have already spread themselves across the surrounding countryside. They don't have time to dawdle in traffic, as they have a busy day ahead of them, working hard to find enough food before, once more, they return in the late afternoon to their communal roost, full of noisy news of the day's events.

Like the corvids, I have headed out from my roosting area and into the wider countryside, but unlike them I have not shared the purpose of my visit with others. Like the birds, though, I do partake of a bit of networking, visiting relatives; but then, as the day draws on and after a bit of a drive, I get to my real destination. Leaving the car behind and wrapped up in my fleece, I strike off down a track that is camleted[97] with the miniature rivers of last night's rain. All around there is wetness, every twig ends in a drip; it is the wettest it can be without actually raining. I leave the track and its watery veins, pushing through the wetness of the laurel leaves that provide an obscuring border between path and woodland beyond.

It has been a while since I last saw it, but the old hornbeam is still there, surrounded by a multitude of struggling conifers, trees that can never, to my mind, compete with it. Hornbeams are beautiful trees, a largely unknown native species; they are actually quite common, growing where the soils are heavy in woodlands as well as often being planted in urban areas, where their grace and autumn colour are used to adorn our streets.

But this is no decorative street tree; it is a woodland survivor that has struggled to cope with the light strangulation of the conifers around it, forcing it to compete. That competition has left its mark on the tree's form; its main trunk is branch-free for several metres – but it is not straight; it is twisted and warped, sculptured by its historical struggle for the light. The silvery bark looks like a thin veil barely containing the pent-up strength of the wood beyond it, ligneous muscles bulging within.

The muscle analogy is a good one for this tree, for its timber is incredibly tough and strong, a strength that is reflected in the tree's name: 'hornbeam' means hard wood. Cutting through its timber is not easy work; a chainsaw will feel blunt as it labours its way through, and the difficulty in working it means that this wood was rarely used in turnery or joinery. But its toughness did lead it to be used where strength was vital. Items as diverse as butcher's blocks and the large wooden cogs in old flour mills were made from its wood, but its greatest use was as a high-quality firewood. Before coal was readily available, the forests of Epping and Hainault that fringe the city of London used to supply hornbeam firewood to fuel the ovens and the furnaces of the growing metropolis. The wood of the hornbeam is the most calorific of British trees, meaning it burns far hotter than logs from other species.

---

97 'Camleted' = having a surface marked with wavy veins.

But hornbeams don't just produce high calorific fuel for us; they also provide calorie-rich fuel for other species, and one of those is the reason why I am here. I leave the old hornbeam and head for another area, where a clump of younger examples grow in a scrubby open area, an area fringed by tall oaks that were drawn up by a conifer crop long since felled. The hornbeams may be younger here, but they are still mature, producing seed; and this year they have produced lots of it. This year has been a mast year, a year of bumper arboreal abundance: the oaks have produced huge quantities of acorns, the ash along the lanes that head out from the village are still covered with bunches of keys, and here it is plain to see that the hornbeams have followed suit.

Bunches of their tri-lobed seeds hang at the end of bare branches, giving the tree a winter silhouette that is not dissimilar to the ash trees around the village. It is these seeds that provide the fuel, a fuel that is chosen as a last meal of the day before roosting. There is a loose flock of several birds moving around the trees, all feeding up ahead of the long night to come: they are mainly siskins and a few lesser redpolls – small finches, beautiful birds in their own right – but I am after a bigger finch.

It has been half an hour since I arrived at this spot, but still they haven't shown. the siskins and redpolls interspersed with coal tits have kept me entertained, but my thoughts begin to drift to the walk back to the car and the ensuing drive home.

But then I look up at the sky, and the unmistakable shapes of three hawfinch fly right over where I am standing. These are the finches I have been waiting for. These chunky, stocky finches show all their diagnostic features as they fly towards the hornbeams: a large heavy-looking head, broad wings and a tail that looks like it has been accidentally cut short, the white curved under-wing markings and white tip to the disproportionate tail emphasising their characteristic shape further.

They fly arrow-straight towards the hornbeams and land in them, swiftly followed by another two. I watch them feed on the hanging seeds, their huge bills making short work of processing them, separating out the seed from its papery winged case. The bill of the hawfinch is a mighty tool, evolved to crack open cherry stones and even, in the south of Europe, the rock-solid stones of wild olives. Here it may appear to be a blunt instrument, a proverbial sledgehammer for the nut, but watching them feed on the hornbeam you can see that it is also perfectly adapted for softer-packaged seeds like these.

Hawfinches are hard birds to get to grips with in Britain; they like to spend much of the time feeding high in the treetops, obscured by the leaves of spring and summer. Their breeding range is poorly known, and there may well be several discrete populations scattered across the country that are unknown to us. But at this time of the year, with their ranks swelled by birds from elsewhere, they can be a bit easier to see, although you still need to know where to look. They form favoured roost sites, and where I am looking is one of them, albeit a rather small one. Their presence here isn't guaranteed, though, but the draw of the abundant hornbeam seed, a real favourite of theirs, helps to increase the chances of seeing these attractive birds as they prepare to roost for the night. There are no leaves now to obscure them, giving me an unhindered view of a bird that certainly deserves to be seen more often.

I watch them for some time, but conscious of the time and the light I finally tear myself away from our largest finch and head back to the car. Walking back I ponder whether the hawfinch roost is as socially interactive as the rook and jackdaw roost I passed at the beginning of the day. Is there an exchange of information, or are they just roosting together for warmth and security? There is so much about our birds that we still know nothing about.

A winter dip

The confused tangle of twisted scruffy branches radiating in all directions creates the instantly identifiable silhouette of a hawthorn, a tree as recognisable in the bare mid-winter as it is in the spring when bedecked with its abundant flowering blossom. How and why this tree has escaped the incessant depredations of the moor's sheep is a mystery, but escape it has, reaching up through the heather, seeking the freedom to become what it should be: a tree. I soon reach, and pass, this campaign-hardened survivor, leaving it to stand in defiance of the odds, high up and isolated on the moor as I continue my trek through its domain.

The hillside opposite me has a patchy covering of straggly gorse bushes, some proudly standing tall, others bent double, collapsing back down to the soil from whence they came. Descending through this labyrinthine mosaic, I watch a fox trot, dancing its way through the spiky green, offering me only brief glimpses of its orange-red and grey winter's coat. A handful of rabbits scatter from the gorse, unnerved by their perennial pursuer, but the fox doesn't seem interested, ignoring their white scuts and continuing its descent into the valley below. I continue my descent, too, but with far less grace than the vulpine dancer, following the rough stony track as it drops down through the moorland towards the river crossing, appreciating the apricity on my way. The blue sky above is gradually being filled in, the white clouds increasingly turning a greyer shade; to the west, the usual source of our weather, a glowering bank of cloud is building up against the landscape dam that is the highest ridge of the moor, the sky, currently held back by the granite bulk that is topped with Yes Tor and High Willhays, foretelling the rain that will inevitably come.

I follow the path downwards until it comes to cross the crystal-clear river, but I don't bridge its flow; instead I head off through the rough vegetation and scattered granite along the river's side, wading through the decaying remains of the summer's bracken, following the river downstream, accompanying the cold, clean water as it rolls off the high ground. The river is fast-flowing, fuelled by the rain-soaked uplands, but this stretch is relatively calm, a low-gradient descent, combined with a good depth, allowing the water to flow through without turbulence. But it is turbulence that I seek. Not for me smooth flowing water. I seek disorder in the passing of the river, boiling commotion, confused clamorous motion.

After a hundred or so metres I find my turbulence. The terrain around me suddenly gets steeper and the river follows suit. The granite rocks breaking through its surface get more numerous and the depth becomes erratic; deep pools and shallow riffling sections intermingle to form a noisy passage for the water to fight its way through. The water's easy flow further upstream has now become a tortuous battle. I settle down on an appropriately shaped piece of granite, ready to wait. But I don't need to wait; within seconds of sitting, there is a loud sharp repeated call cutting through the background noise of the water, and a bird rushes past on blurred wing beats, an arrow-straight flight terminating on a rock that sticks out midstream about 20 metres from where I am sitting. The dipper lands on its granite islet, dips its legs in true dipper fashion and then walks straight into the fast-pouring water.

Quickly moving cold moorland water is no barrier for these aquatic birds, and the dipper quickly disappears from my view as it immerses itself in the flow. A few seconds pass and it emerges in the shallows on the far side of the river before turning and entering the waters again. The dipper is one of our most specialist birds, perfectly adapted for this life of entering fast-flowing moorland streams and rivers. This bird's skeleton is not made up of the normal light, honeycombed hollow bones so characteristic of flying birds; its bones are dense and solid, reducing the bird's buoyancy and adding extra weight to it – extra weight that may explain its fast, whirring wing action when flying. Those wings that seem to struggle to keep the bird aloft in the air are also used to propel it along underwater, becoming penguin-like flippers, converting flyer to swimmer. Its strong feet, topped with sharp claws, help it to grip to the stream bed as it enters the water, the proportionally long legs helping it to resist the flow.

Searching for tiny aquatic insect larvae under the water requires good eyesight, but seeing under water and seeing above it are two very different things, so the remarkable dipper changes the curvature of its eye lenses as it enters the liquid medium in which it seeks its food, enabling it to focus as clearly when submerged as it can back out on the surface. The bird's insect prey tends to hide away under stones and debris, requiring a thorough search to find them, but searching takes time, and time runs out fast when you have to hold your breath. But even though this is a small bird, roughly the size of a starling, it is able to hold its breath for up to 30 seconds, giving it the time required to seek, find and snatch its aquatic food.

The bird re-emerges onto the original rock that it first landed on, its densely feathered and well-oiled plumage looking dry as soon as it leaves the water. It flexes those knees again, dipping down a couple of times – and then it's off, whirry wings blurring its shape as it flies away downstream. I remain where I am, prepared to wait patiently for another view of this birding marvel, but a quick glance towards Yes Tor persuades me otherwise. The greying sky has become a blackening sky. Reluctantly I decide to leave, disappointed that my visit has been cut short, but delighted with my Dartmoor dippering.

I cut across the vegetation, making for the track, upsetting some sheep grazing the flora hard, and causing a raven to cronk at me from above as if admonishing me for

A dipper having a dip in a Dartmoor river.

deviating from the path. As I watch the large black bird riding the increasing wind with ease, I feel the first heavy drops of rain hit me. By the time I get back to the car I am soaked. My expensive waterproofs have kept the majority of the water out, but they are evidently no match for the impermeable plumage of the little dipper.

Hacked rats

I retrieve the trail camera from the garden on a cold morning, eagerly opening the case to get at the controls within. I love putting the camera out, and I am always excited to see what I have recorded, to see what has been using our garden overnight. The grainy footage on the camera's small screen reveals a true-life story of a mammal's dexterity; it shows it climbing up the vertical trunk of the goat willow with consummate ease, it shows it travelling nonchalantly along the wrist-thick branch of the pollarded tree until it reaches the end and then hangs downward, its rear legs tightly holding the branch whilst grabbing at the suspended fat balls in their cage below with its front limbs.

The ecstatic delight I would feel if it was a mustelid performing such a feat – a stoat, say, or an unlikely marten – would be unbounded. The level of cuteness if it were a wood mouse, all big ears and twitching nose, would be off the scale. Wry grins all around at the

Winter

137

cheekiness of a grey squirrel if it were he or she – but no, the mammal on my trail camera footage is none of these. It is a rat. A big brown rat.

When it comes to wildlife and our perceptions of it, image is everything. Looking at my recorded video, I should be admiring the ingeniousness of this rodent, praising its skill at climbing a vertical trunk, watching in awe at its gravity-defying agility as it hangs by its back legs to reach the food below. Instead, my first thought was along the lines of 'Oh great, we've got bloody rats.' When it comes to image, it is fair to say that rats have something of a problem.

We don't like to admit it, most of us prefer not to think of it, but the brown rat is always with us; it just keeps out of our way, very rarely showing itself, living a subterranean existence for much of the time and generally venturing out after dark when it makes excursions above ground. The winter is the time that we tend to see them: the vegetation has died back and more of us have bird food out and available, particularly fat balls.

The brown rat is one of Britain's commonest mammals, with some estimates suggesting that it even outnumbers us humans.[98] It is a not a native mammal, though; coming originally from central Asia, it found its way here following human travellers, probably arriving on our shores only as recently as the 1720s, a date that is long after the event that it is often blamed for, the Black Death. That plague first struck Britain in the 14th century, killing at least a third of the human population, and outbreaks of the lethal pestilence reoccurred periodically after that date, with the last serious outbreak, known as the Great Plague of London, occurring in the 1660s, some sixty or so years before a brown rat had even set foot here.

The brown rat has become the unwitting fall guy in the plague story: in the eyes of many a rat is a rat, and therefore it was behind the Black Death. But it wasn't. It was another species of rat – or rather its fleas – that were the probable source of this lethal disease: the black rat, a species now critically endangered, if not extinct, in Britain. The black rat, like its brown relative, is also originally from Asia, but it quickly spread when our trading became global, following the commerce, and colonising Europe and Britain on the back of the Roman Empire. If we want to blame a rat for the plague, we should be blaming the black rat, not the brown. But even that is being simplistic, with modern studies now showing that there was another major spreader of the plague within Europe: us, *Homo sapiens*, and our very own motley collection of fleas and lice.

Of course, just because it wasn't the actual species of rat involved in the spread of the Black Death, it doesn't mean that the brown rat hasn't caused us problems: they are notorious raiders and spoilers of food stocks, and they do spread disease, including the unpleasant leptospirosis or Weil's disease. They are also part of the complex pathological path of toxoplasmosis, a disease that often infects humans via our pet cats. The remarkable parasite that is responsible for the disease, *Toxoplasma gondii*, spends the early part of its life living within the brown rat; but to reproduce, to continue its genetic lineage, it has

---

98 There is no official number of rats in the UK, but some estimates are around the 80 million mark: about 1.3 rats per human.

to get itself into a domestic cat's body. There is an obvious pathway for the parasite to follow: if it can get a cat to predate the rat, then the transfer from body to body, species to species, can take place. But for the parasite, it isn't about getting a cat to predate the rat; it is about getting the rat to be predated by the cat.

Studies[99] have shown that the parasite doesn't get into the cat by chance; instead it manipulates its host, the rat, to behave in such a way that it increases its chances of being predated by a cat. A parasite so small that we need a powerful microscope to see it is actually programming the rat, hacking into its central nervous system so that it can make the rat do what the parasite needs it to do. It sounds like something out of a science fiction thriller, but it is very much real life. Rats aren't highly successful for nothing; they have evolved traits to avoid undue risk, and a good example of this is that they have an aversion to areas where there are signs of the presence of domestic cats. Rats perceive the risk and adjust their behaviour accordingly.

But this is no good for the parasite; it needs to get to the cat, so it actually changes the brain of the rat, it manipulates the animal's behaviour, it reprograms the animal's brain, reducing its perception of the risk and making it behave in a reckless manner in areas where cats are found. In other words, this microscopic hacker gets its host eaten by its next host.

I find this, if you'll excuse the unintended pun, absolutely mind-blowing. When I re-watch the footage I try to work out if I am watching the behaviour of a healthy opportunistic rodent or the behaviour of a programmed food parcel. Rats and brain-hacking parasites might not be everybody's cup of tea, but they are a great example of just how amazing the natural world around us is.

Festive delights

Christmas day dawns clear with a slight breath of frost that has touched the windscreens of the cars parked along the street outside. A dunnock, with its rattling song, accompanies a robin in welcoming the new day; their songs intermingle, a collection of clear and crisp notes. It is the first time that I have heard a dunnock sing this winter. The robin famously sings throughout the autumn and winter, but the less showy dunnock will also sing in the colder months, often starting up around the turn of the year and gradually increasing the frequency of its singing activity as spring approaches. This bird is a bit early, but I am not complaining; perhaps the low winter sun has spurred it on to provide a Christmas treat for those of us that can hear its tumbling melody.

The sun has spurred me on too, and I have decided on a Christmas morning walk before the overeating begins – a quick saunter along the lanes before returning to the warmth of home. I head out of the village without seeing a soul, walking quickly along the narrow roads. I stop on the old stone bridge where the lane crosses the river, my attention caught by the purple-toned catkins and small black cones decorating the alder branches that hang over the turbid, turbulent muddy waters of the river below. The clear

---

99 'Fatal attraction in rats infected with *Toxoplasma gondii*', Berdoy et al, *Journal of the Royal Society*, 2000.

languid flow of the summer is now nothing but a memory: the swollen river has been up over its banks, flattening vegetation, with flotsam stranded in lower branches and large irregular shallow lakes of water on the fields all testament to the last few days of seemingly endless rain. The sky above has once again clouded over, a blanket of grey replacing the earlier expanse of blue, but there is no threat of further precipitation within it; it is not a dark threatening grey, rather a soft grey, dull in colour and dull in action, dulling the light and the colours of the winter landscape.

But not even the sky and its subdued blanket of grey can dim the bright white of the bird that stands within one of the shallow stranded waters of the river's overspill lakes. A little egret stands in the water, its soap-powder-advert plumage suitably immaculate amongst the dull greens and browns that surround it. The bird's neck is stretched out, its elevated head perfectly still as it watches the water in which it stands with an intense glare, waiting for a movement to betray a stranded opportunity for a meal.

This small heron may now be a common sight in Britain, especially here in Devon, but there is still something brilliantly incongruous about this spotlessly white bird standing in the middle of a sodden field on a grey winter's morning. It is a Christmas

Little egrets are now common birds and are regularly encountered, but this doesn't detract from their glory.

treat for me to behold and to enjoy; these are birds that, for me at least, always cause excitement, birds that always look exotic even though they are not. I revel in the quiet beauty of the scene and the bird's white beauty for several minutes, neither of us moving, the bird intently staring whilst I am filled with joy. The small fish, cut off from the river and trapped in the shallow pools, waiting for a further deluge to bring them salvation, probably don't share in my joy of the bird's presence.

I leave the egret to its vigil, walking back up the lane and feeling pleased with myself as I walk, buoyed by the bird that I have just been watching. Chuckling fieldfares fly by overhead and a great spotted woodpecker bounces over the valley: Christmas gifts to go with the song of the dunnock and the robin, and the image of the egret.

The new year dawns and with it another couple of birds add their songs to those of the dunnock and the robin: the first is the house sparrow, a male chirping monotonously from the bramble and honeysuckle tangle in which they seem to spend so much time. It is a background sort of song, one that isn't instantly noticeable – but the other bird's song is most certainly not background. An explosion of melody finished off with a flourish comes from the wren on top of the wall. Tail cocked upright, it looks around itself before unleashing another incredibly loud salvo of its beautiful song. The beginning of the year signifies the beginning of territorial establishment for this small bird, and as if to confirm this another wren sings from a couple of gardens away. They are laying claim to their territories, both to ensure they have access to enough foraging in these cold winter months and to put down a marker for the spring. This vocalised staking of their territorial claims will increase from this point on. It is without doubt an audible pleasure for us, but it is a very serious business for the wrens.

The feeders are busy with coal tits and blue tits, whilst a wood pigeon shuffles along underneath, hoovering up any spillage. A beautiful male greenfinch, looking absolutely resplendent, lands on top of the metal holder from which the feeders hang; it surveys the comings and goings of the much smaller tits below it before dropping down on to one of the pegs and helping itself to the seeds within. Unlike the tits, the greenfinch doesn't waste time or energy flying back and forth, it has stationed itself at the feeder and there it remains for several minutes, calmly feeding away while the smaller birds are a literal blur of activity around it.

The bills of the tits have evolved primarily for feeding on small insects hidden amongst the leaves and twigs of trees and shrubs. They are small and fine, ideal for winkling out a caterpillar from amongst the foliage, but not so great for cleaving open a sunflower seed. The tits fly into the feeder, snatch a seed and then fly off again so that they can go and open it elsewhere; perching on a branch they hold the seed in one of their feet and then jab at it with their bill, pecking it open. The greenfinch, though, doesn't need to do this; it has a bill that is perfect for the job in hand.

A male greenfinch glows in the winter light.

Sitting at the feeder, it picks up a seed with its hefty beak and macerates it open with ease, using its tongue to flick the seed into its mouth whilst the discarded husks fall to the floor below. It has no need to find a perch where it can safely hold the seed in its feet and peck it open; instead it can sit and dominate its side of the feeder, safe in the knowledge that no tit is big enough to challenge it for the food within. After about a minute and a half of feeding, the male greenfinch is evidently sated. It pauses for a moment, looking about the garden with a calm air to it, in perfect contrast to the tits flashing past it constantly on a blur of hurried wings, and then it opens its own wings, flashing yellow and green as it goes; this miniature garden parrot of a bird flies up and over the wall, seeking the cover of the huge laurel beyond.

The blackbirds have departed the garden now; with the berries of the hawthorn and the ivy now depleted, they have moved on to search for nourishment elsewhere. It is the first time for a long time that our garden is blackbirdless, and I'm already missing them.

A percussive message

A breeze arises from an unknown source, flowing like a river through the canopies of the pine above me, tossing them about in the sudden white-water air. Occasional waves escape the main flow, diverting outwards until they lap up against the beech on the far side of the plantation, rattling their bare branches noisily. And then, as suddenly as it appeared, the river of air is gone, leaving only a ripple of memory playing through the grey-green needles of the tall pines.

It takes a moment for the avian activity of the canopy to begin again; the sudden wind stilled the bird life, but with the wind vanishing as quickly as it arrived, the miniature feathered movements restart. Inevitably it is the coal tits that first catch the eye with their busy forays amongst the paired needles, gleaning them for invertebrates as they hang by their pin-thin legs from the slenderest of branches, the bold white mark on the backs of their heads highlighting their movements in amongst the dull grey-green of the Scots pine's narrow leaves. These small members of the tit family are always on the go; primarily a bird of coniferous woodland, they have been quick to follow their more familiar cousins into our gardens, readily exploiting our seed feeders in their endless quest for nourishment. Small birds have a greater surface area to volume ratio: what this means is that small birds lose body heat quicker than bigger birds. With the coal tit being so small, the winter months bring a stiff challenge for it: can it find enough food to fuel its calorific needs? If it doesn't it perishes, and this is the reason it is always busy, because, quite simply, it has to be busy to survive. We get them in the garden throughout the year, but in the winter their numbers increase dramatically, with dozens targeting the sunflower seeds, rapidly depleting the feeding tubes with their constant activity.

If you watch coal tits at your feeders first thing in the morning, you will notice that after an initial burst of frenetic feeding to help them regain the bodyweight they lost the night before, they switch their activity from feeding to caching. They start to store the seeds they are gathering. This is a good strategy for a bird that has to feed regularly to maintain its body warmth; just because there is seed present now doesn't mean that there will be later, so the ability to store it for leaner times is a good one. Sunflower seeds are basically 50 per cent fat, so are the ideal fuel for a small bird like the coal tit, and an ideal way for the bird to build up its fat reserves ahead of yet another long cold winter's night. These small birds are prolific storers of sunflower seeds, but they also seem quite forgetful about where they store them. We have sunflowers growing everywhere in our garden, all planted by these small tits: they bury them in plant pots and jam them into crevices in the stone wall, into the gaps in the wooden steps, into the bark of the hawthorn and even into our thatch! Pale green shoots of the emerging plants pop up everywhere; most of them are killed off by the frosts, but some survive and we usually have two or three that we allow to grow on. If you ever find an unplanned sunflower growing in your garden, it is highly likely that a coal tit was responsible for planting it.

The coal tit is the source of many sunflowers!

The pines above me have no sunflower seeds, but they evidently have an abundance of something for these tiny acrobatic birds, their constant activity in those trees a reflection of the food availability. Another bird catches my eye as it flies diagonally downwards, landing on the trunk of one of the evenly spaced pines before immediately scampering, mouselike, up the first couple of feet of it. It is a treecreeper, one of the best-named birds we have. It pauses in its treecreeping to probe its slender curved tweezer-like bill into a furrow in the tree's bark, carefully extracting a small protein-packed invertebrate before creeping upwards again, spiralling around the tree's tall straight branchless stem, vanishing from sight before appearing once more several feet higher up. Just when you begin to think that this small bird is actually more small-mammal-like in behaviour, it drops off the trunk of the tree, opening its wings and flashing its white underside as it flies diagonally downwards again, to land at the base of another trunk a few trees away, from where the scampering ascent begins anew. There is something mesmerising about watching a feeding treecreeper, watching it run up a trunk, probing as it goes, before watching it fly back down to another stem and then watching it creep its way up that one too. Up down, up down, up down, a hypnotic rhythm of avian action.

In my near-trancelike treecreeper viewing, I almost miss the significance of the sound that just about reaches my consciousness – a mere shadow of a sound, really, but one that has me breaking my hypnotic treecreeper watching to strain my ears. I hear it again, the faint but distinctive drumming that heralds a change in the seasons:

The drumming of the great spotted woodpecker is the signal of yet more seasonal change. (Photo by kind permission of Stuart Gillies.)

a great spotted woodpecker performing a high-speed drumroll, a blur of percussive sound that reverberates around the forest. It sounds a long way off, but its significance is unmistakable: winter is receding, spring is coming and the woodpecker is laying down its territorial claim for the forthcoming season with its rapid morse code-like message.

Many of us have our favourite natural sounds. I have many: blackbirds singing on a warm spring evening, chiffchaffs tunelessly announcing their March return, the deep drone of a hornet zipping past me, the curt bark of a roe buck on a humid summer evening. There are so many, so many, that make me feel great when I hear them again for the first time each year. The drumroll of the great spotted woodpecker on a late January day is most definitely one of them.

Returning favourites and favourites to return to

I opened the back door three days ago to find a male blackbird sitting on the herb bed wall just a foot or so away from me. He wasn't alarmed at my sudden appearance; in fact it was as though he had been expecting it. Could this be the young male that had adopted us in the autumn? He cocked his head to look at me and I in turn took a good look at him. He looked beautiful, a typical male blackbird, but as I looked more closely at him I noticed that his feathers still had a hint of brownness about them, that his yellow bill had a remnant of blackness left close to where it meets the head: telltale signs of a youngster newly moulted into adult plumage.

He was sitting exactly where the young male used to sit when awaiting his food last autumn. I grabbed some mealworms and went to feed him; sure enough the bird stepped back onto the soil in exactly the same way as the youngster used to do, allowing me to put the food down. I watched him feed, scattering particles of mealworm all over the place, and then watched as he turned, hopped across the soil and onto the large pot that is home to a perpetual kale. He then flew up to the top of the steps, had a pause, looked about and then ran over the granite gravel to the base of the bird bath before flying up onto it for a drink. It is exactly what the young male did last year. It has to be him. Our youngster has come home. I cannot begin to describe the elation that that brings.

Over the last few days the male blackbird has quickly settled back into the garden and into the routine of exploiting us for food. With the colder temperatures the back door is now shut, but the bird still comes looking for us and his mealworms, and he has started to fly up to the kitchen window sill where he sits and peers in. Slightly perturbed by the bird flying in very close to the concussion-hard glass, I have constructed a small perch for him to land on instead. He has taken to it straightaway, landing on it and looking in at us in the kitchen, attracting our attention and getting his reward of mealworms. He is still doing his quiet little song, sitting on the perch in front of the window and singing away with closed beak. I really hope he will use that perch to give us the full, unmuted, version in the spring.

Our friend the blackbird on its perch at the kitchen window awaiting yet more food!

The natural world is a tough place; it's hard, there is no room for sentiment. But there is room for sentiment in our own lives, and if I want to believe that this blackbird is my friend, then sod it I *will* believe it. It brings me such joy when he appears on the perch; he may be interrupting me as I write away at the kitchen table, but I don't care – in fact I look forward to it. There are some naturalists that will look down their noses at my behaviour, but I am a naturalist because I love nature, I enjoy it, it makes me feel good. I feel connected to this blackbird, I enjoy being at his beck and call, helping to supplement his diet, helping him to survive, but I also, completely selfishly, enjoy how his presence makes me feel.

I would write more, but he is sitting on the perch looking at me.

Whenever I am heading north on the M5 motorway, I always try and fit in a quick stop just past the M4/M5 interchange, a break in the journey, a pause. But this is no usual service station pause; it is actually more of a pilgrimage, a trip to see an old friend, a friend that doesn't even know me, a friend that has been revered and visited by travellers for many a century.

The Tortworth Chestnut, a great sprawling arboreal mass, is just five minutes' diversion from the motorway, but it is a whole world away in reality. What a tree it is! Now, at this time of year, naked and exposed without its suit of long green leaves, it can be seen in all of its architectural arboreal glory. It is a riot of unregulated growth, long-collapsed limbs pullulating forth once more from where they have sunk to the ground, it is a three-dimensional tangle of ligneous wonder, everything from massive spiral-fissure-barked trunks to the finger-thin knobbly twigs of last year's growth. This is a tree of complete unconformity. Arboreal anarchy in the UK.

Just how long it has grown here is a matter of conjecture, and for some it is the source of much debate, but to me this tree's age is not important; it is a number that's irrelevant when you are standing in the grass looking at it whilst a few miles away a transport artery pumps countless vehicles around on their equally irrelevant journeys. Sweet chestnuts aren't native to Britain, but their culinary usefulness has long led to them being transported and propagated by humans – how long no one knows for sure, but as a species it has probably been here since Roman times. I have seen an even bigger and older chestnut – a colossal– growing in its native range of southern Europe, a massive old behemoth of a tree whose continued existence is even more remarkable considering it grows on the lower slopes of the world's most active volcano, Etna in Sicily.[100]

Veteran trees have a fascination for many, including me; their vast age, often incalculable, is an obvious reason, but there is also the doggedness of the individual that appeals, the sheer bloodymindedness of it to survive all that nature and ourselves have thrown at it over the countless years. We might not have active volcanoes in Britain, but

---

100 The Hundred Horse Sweet Chestnut is found in the town of Sant'Alfio in Sicily.

Winter

The arboreal magnificence that is the Tortworth Chestnut.

Incredibly this is all just one tree, the largest sweet chestnut in the world, growing on the slopes of Mount Etna in Sicily, with the author for scale. (Photo by Jo Parsons.)

we are an overcrowded island with immense pressures on the land and its uses, so we are as damaging as any lava flow, as reckless as any pyroclastic surge. But still the Tortworth Chestnut survives and grows, pouring out new growth every spring, cloaking the ground beneath it in dense shade every summer, and standing strong against the autumn and winter storms.

It sits behind a short wooden fence at the back of a grassy area offset from the local church. I suspect that it draws more visitor veneration than the building does, and it is certainly a tree that deserves to be worshipped. I love just standing looking at it, especially from the little path on the side; from here you can clearly see the remnant hulk of the original stem and its long-dead branches, bleached wooden reminders of many a century of weather, one of them spiralling upwards like a corkscrew. From this viewpoint you can see two mighty stems, looking like trees of their own, growing to the right of the original – two towering trunks reaching upwards – and on the other side another large stem grows from low down on the side of the old hulk, angling outwards, telling the tale of how it chased the light when it first grew.

When I stand looking at this tree, time seems to be inconsequential. My own lifetime is recorded in just a very small percentage of the annual rings that it has laid down. For me, travelling as I am, this tree is the ultimate pause in the journey. There are no tasteless, scalding hot and ridiculously expensive coffees to be had, no flashing arcade machines to rest your weary eyes on, no shops to sell you an inflatable neck pillow you'll never use – but this tree, this brilliant, awe-inspiring tree, is the best service station in the country.

Relaxed and refreshed by the arboreal glory that is the Tortworth Chestnut, I return to the car, content and ready to continue on my journey.

Foxy attitudes

The sharp, acrid, but somehow pleasing, smell of a fox hangs heavy in the cold air, an olfactory calling card left by a vulpine carnivore. Scent always seems stronger to me on cold still mornings, but we humans don't use smell as our primary sense, so for this pungent aroma to be so noticeable to me, so strong, implies that its source has only very recently been liberally applied to the path edge.

The red fox is regarded as a rural animal; it has become something of a cultural meme that for any story set in the countryside a fox should be included somewhere in it. This can be as a crafty character in a children's tale, or as a barking vixen providing the soundtrack to a dark night in the murder-rich area of Midsomer. If you are a children's writer or a television crime drama producer, nothing says 'rural' like a fox.

Our village is in a rural area, located right in the heart of the rural county of Devon, but we very rarely see a fox around the village, and when we do it is invariably lying dead at the side of the road. We see the odd one on the moor. But if we want to experience some foxy viewing then it is not a rural location we head for but the city; foxes are an abundant urban animal in Britain.[101] I can remember driving through the Poole/

---

101 It is believed that there are around 150,000 urban foxes in Britain.

Bournemouth conurbation late at night many years ago, and being thrilled and amazed at the number of foxes I saw. They were everywhere. At the time I was employed as a forest ranger out in the Dorset countryside, and I never saw foxes where I worked or where I lived, but there in the urban sprawl that is home to over 390,000 people, these beautiful opportunists were everywhere.

It is because they are such opportunists that they are found in such high numbers in our urban areas; indeed the highest densities of foxes anywhere in Britain are found in cities and towns rather than the rural idyll in which their image places them. The reason is that the red fox is hard to see in most rural areas, yet is easier to see in many urban areas. It is, of course, us humans and our attitudes that dictate how the fox behaves. Foxes are generally not liked in rural areas; they are seen as predators that can damage our interests – and indeed a fox getting into a chicken coop brings not only death to the chickens but also heartbreak to the humans that own them. There can be no denying that the fox is a predator, and that it will take any opportunity to kill our chickens etc, but the fox is pursued and persecuted in many rural districts regardless of whether it is harming anyone's interests. It is pursued and persecuted for just being what it is: a fox.

This continued threat could keep a fox population below the level that the rural environment can support, but it also alters the behaviour of the foxes. They become more wary; if every time they see a human that human tries to cause it harm, then the fox will soon learn not to be seen, to become an unobtrusive lurker that eschews human contact. But in the urban environment, where humans aren't generally allowed to carry guns or set traps, the foxes benefit from the more benevolent attitude towards them. In some cases this attitude is indifferent, the fox of no more interest to the city or town dweller than next door's cat. But in other cases the attitude is welcoming; people enjoy seeing these wild animals in their midst, they enjoy sharing their tame environment with something that is a connection to their image of wildness. Some people go further than just enjoying seeing foxes, they actively encourage them into their gardens by feeding them, a behaviour that would be anathema to some rural dwellers. Whether the attitude is one of indifference or is friendly, the urban foxes soon learnt that humans weren't something they needed to continuously hide away from; indeed they soon realised that they could exploit humans and the human environment for their own needs.

Urban foxes have a rubbish diet, quite literally. When it comes to food we are incredibly wasteful: it has been reported that households in the UK throw away 4.5 million tonnes of food a year[102] and that isn't including the fast food that gets left on our town and city centre streets every Friday and Saturday night. It is no wonder that an opportunist animal such as the fox soon learnt to exploit this bonanza of feeding opportunity that we and our habits provide.

But it is not all junk food for the fox; our cities provide a wealth of safe green spaces for them as well, and it is within one of these spaces that I am standing when I breathe in the strong signature scent of the fox. I am in Higher Cemetery in the city

102 *The Guardian*, 24 January 2020.

of Exeter, a great place to come if like me you are a dendrophile or tree lover, as it is an arboretum of sorts, with a whole host of tree species from all around the world that mix in perfectly with the graves of a whole host of people from around the world. It is also a large area of green that is a stone's throw away from a park, a playing field, allotments and a railway cutting, all surrounded by houses and their gardens, all of them great places for a fox.

There will be lots of voles and mice for the fox to predate, and there will be earthworms and invertebrates to harvest as well as seasonal delights such as blackberries to enjoy. It may be that the fox I can smell feeds on a near-natural diet, although I suspect the attraction of our food waste is too strong for it to ignore. There are sheds aplenty for the fox to create its den under; it seems a perfect place for this canid to reside. It isn't completely safe of course – the roads and the railways take their toll – but the levels of persecution and the concomitant risk of untimely death are incredibly low compared to those that their rural cousins face.

As I wander through the trees, testing my ID knowledge on the winter buds and getting myself all confused by a liquidambar, I get a glimpse of the source of the strong scent. At the bottom of the slope, flitting in and out of view behind the leaning tombstones, a fox is walking briskly along. Although its pace is quick, it seems relaxed and untroubled as it lithely picks its way through the reminders of past lives. Foxes are great to watch, and their fluid movements are easy on the eye, but I only get to enjoy it for a brief time. Finished with the open space of the graveyard, the fox effortlessly slips through a hedge and vanishes into the world of suburban gardens beyond. I am left with a happy memory of it as I continue to contemplate the arboreal puzzles of the cemetery.

Winter is a busy time for foxes, wherever they live. The females come into oestrus and it is during the months of January and February that the vixen can often be heard summoning males with her long drawn out, somewhat haunting, call, the very call so beloved of television producers. As I stand in the cemetery looking at the multitude of houses around it, I wonder what their residents think as they hear this eerie call emanating from the darkness of the graveyard beyond their fences. I feel a tinge of jealousy as I stand there: I don't get to hear the call when I am standing in my own garden deep in rural Devon.

Freezing encounters

It is cold. A low air temperature combined with an easterly breeze is always a bitterly cold mix. It's precisely the sort of day to spend indoors with the heating on, not the sort of day to be sitting in a bird hide on an estuary. But that is exactly where I am, having eschewed the creature comforts of home for the hard wooden bench and sparsity of the hide. I'm not the only one; others are here, too, wrapped up in a multitude of layers, birders with woollen hats pulled tightly down over their heads, peering through expensive optics, contemplating reaching for another hot drink from the obligatory stainless steel flask that accompanies each of us.

The sky above is a watered-down blue. There is no trace of warmth in it, and the low sun casts a bright light through the dry easterly air. The visibility is crystal clear. These are great bird-watching conditions, even if it is bloody cold. In front of the hide, crowds of wigeon and teal sit on the grassy islands, some huddled together with their heads tucked into their bodies. But others are hardier, swimming in the partially iced waters, their chests breaking the thin layer of frozen liquid as they propel themselves along. They are the feathered ice-breakers of the marsh.

A large gaggle of geese are further out across the artificially flooded land; the large greylags are busy mowing the long grasses, whilst the smaller Brent geese are grouped together on the large body of open water. In amongst the Brent are hundreds of ducks: there are shovel-beaked shoveler ducks sitting low in the water, and there are also the black and white tufteds, birds that seem to dive at the exact same moment that you get your binoculars on them, leaving you with a perfectly focused ripple. Here and there are the magnificently elegant pintails with their eponymous tail pointing behind them as they sit on the open water looking ridiculously graceful. Mallards form large floating groups, serenely gliding along the surface, and in amongst them are a few of the more subdued but subtly beautiful gadwall, unobtrusively going on with their lives. Wigeon and teal are everywhere.

A beautiful male pochard causes a stir of activity in the hide. Several of the hunched-up, wrapped-up birders reach for their cameras in unison as he swims purposefully towards us, offering great views in the low sunlight of his brilliant red head and contrasting black, soft grey- black, body. The telltale clicks of multiple shutters record the admiration in which this duck is held, although some of the clicks are followed by heavy sighs of frustration as the diving duck does exactly that on a regular basis.

Lines of gulls criss-cross the weak blue sky as yet more ducks and geese fly in to escape the peak of the incoming tide on the adjacent estuary, the geese's landings splashing the water and scattering the floating ducks. There are large numbers of geese and ducks, but these numbers pale into insignificance when compared to the numbers of waders that are present.

The turbulent landings of some of the geese upset the relative calm of a mass of loafing godwits, both black-tailed and bar-tailed, causing them to take to the air, flashing their white under-wings as they get lift. The wings and the light turn them from birds into a shimmering low cloud that obscures everything behind them, but this cloud doesn't last long, breaking up and raining the birds back down to the ground – and as they land the mass of light-reflecting white vanishes instantly. There are a few ripples of movement through the mass of godwits, and then they settle down once more, hundreds of birds loafing together, heads tucked in out of the cold, probing wind. As I scan around the

Black-tailed godwits braving the icy conditions.

reserve I can see lots more smaller groups of godwit all doing the same, and dotted about them are individual curlew and even a couple of their smaller relative, the whimbrel. The graceful avocet are also taking time out, standing on their dainty legs with their upcurved bills tucked in out of sight under their wings; high-tide slumbering.

But not all the waders are taking the opportunity to have a rest. Right in front of the hide there are several common redshank, all of them busy scurrying over the watery, grassy edges, probing here and there, always looking for something to eat, something to fuel their energy, to keep the internal fire burning. The beautifully plumaged lapwing are also tireless in their activity, feeding away in the grassy areas and entering into disputes amongst themselves; sometimes they fly up in small groups, flapping black and white as they circle briefly before dropping down just a few yards from where they started. A greenshank is also wide awake, purposefully striding through the shallows, occasionally making a short sharp dash through the water to snaffle a small morsel that catches its eye.

There is so much to look at, so much behaviour to watch and to observe, that you soon forget the icy cold temperature gnawing away at you. Watching three camouflaged snipe probing in a shallow, muddy pool out on the grass is a great way to ignore the fact that your toes feel like individual blocks of ice. A muffled voice from one of the other hide huddlers announces that a water rail has appeared; everybody turns to look, to follow the brief, somewhat parsimonious, directions to the bird. Water rails seem to spend most of their lives in deep cover, hidden by reeds and the like, only revealing their presence with their distinctive squealing stuck-pig call. But in the cold of winter they can sometimes be much more obliging, and this one is being just that, strutting across the grass on the far right-hand side of the reserve. But even though it is in the open, it is steadfastly keeping close to the sedge-lined ditch and unruly hedge that form the boundary, keeping the cover close at hand. In the shadow of the hedge it looks dark, but as it walks about the white underside of the tail occasionally catches enough light to gleam momentarily. The route it is following is somewhat meandering, but it is gradually getting closer to an area of sunlit ground, and several long-lensed cameras are readied in anticipation of this exquisitely marked bird walking forth into the light. But before it gets there it takes fright and turns sharply, scurrying along to a clump of sedge, prompting many dark mutterings from within the hide. When the bird reappears, it seems content to stay within the unphotogenic shade of the hedge.

Suddenly everything is up. Loud alarm calls resound around the marsh as everything seems to take to the air at once. A huge flock of previously unseen dunlin rise up as one, twisting and turning in mesmerising fashion. The godwits do likewise; everything is a mass of confusing movement and flashing plumages. In the hide we all strain forward, trying to see upwards into the blue, trying to spot the cause of the pandemonium in front – surely there is a raptor in the air, a peregrine perhaps. But try as we might, we can't see anything. The trigger for the panic is not obvious to us, and after a few seconds it becomes apparent that it is not obvious, either, to the birds in the sky, which rapidly regain their composure and drop back down to the grass and water of the reserve, settling back into their routines again. By the time any of us in the hide remembers the water rail, it has long returned to its preference for obscurity.

The predicted snow has fallen, muffling everything with its blanket of clean whiteness. For Devon it is quite a fall, maybe 10 or 12 centimetres. The normal flow of traffic on the main road through the village is stilled, but the flow of birds in the garden has dramatically increased and is the heaviest it has been all winter. The snow brings with it birds that we don't normally see in the garden. A treecreeper has been in, feeding on the bark of the hawthorn, and has even been exploring the many nooks and crannies of the stone wall in its desperation for food. A pied wagtail, a bird that is often seen overhead but not within the garden's confines, has dropped in to pick its way around the pond as it too searches for sustenance.

The fat balls and the seed feeders are a blur of feathers. Greenfinch, goldfinch, chaffinch, blue tit, coal tit, great tit, long-tailed tit and house sparrows are all crowding around the feeders; occasionally they get scattered by a nuthatch hurtling in behind its pointed bill. Underneath, dunnock, blackbirds and robin are picking through the debris, whilst a wren hunts the ivy assiduously. I crunch up the snowy steps to top up the feeders, scattering a large quantity of mealworms all around and placing a big fat apple down onto the white snow. As I head back down I spot a redwing sitting in the hawthorn, the first time I have seen one of these in the garden, its stripy head cocked to one side as it watches me walk by underneath.

Within minutes of me getting back into the warmth of the house, a gang of starlings descend on the mealworms that I have just scattered about the snow, nine of them voraciously devouring the dried insect larvae. I head back out to scatter even more, taking with me some warm water, and as I get to the top of the steps I flush another garden first, this time from within the pyracantha: a fieldfare. Feeling pleased to see such a magnificent bird using our garden I quickly knock out the solid block of ice from the bird bath and replace it with the warm water. In freezing conditions such as these access to fresh water is as important for birds as access to food.

I return to the sanctuary of the house and ensconce myself at the back bedroom window. There are several things I could be doing, but watching the birds is what I want to be doing, so that is exactly what I opt to do. The fieldfare returns to the pyracantha. So far this winter, the small yellow berries it bears have been ignored; an abundance of berries in the countryside and the fact that this variety is yellow rather than the more avian-attractive red has meant that it is now well stocked to provide some much-needed nourishment. The large wintering thrush plucks a few of the berries, but its eye is taken by the apple placed in the snow at the top of the steps. It drops down into full view, a beautiful fieldfare, its colours highlighted and framed by the white of the snow lying

The fieldfare with 'its' apple in the foreground.

all around it, just 4 metres away from where I am sitting. It pecks greedily at the apple for several minutes, feeding away, eating its fill. When it stops, I expect it to fly off, but instead, its immediate hunger sated, it hunkers down by the apple, tucking its head into its body and fluffing out its feathers to trap warm air. I realise that it is guarding the fruit.

The apple, which a few minutes before had sat in our wooden fruit bowl, is now a valuable resource for this thrush. By exposing itself on the ground like this as it rests, the bird is taking a calculated risk. There is a risk of predation, but there is also a risk that if the bird flies to a safer place the apple may be gone on its return, and that may mean starvation. This precious food is too great a resource to risk losing, and so the fieldfare settles in to guard it whilst it digests its first sitting. It is a vigilant sentry, not allowing anything within a set distance. The starlings return to feed on the mealworms, but any that lie within a 30-centimetre or so radius of the thrush are out of bounds as far as the bigger bird is concerned. It readily lunges at any starlings that attempt to get closer, despite the fact that they aren't interested in the apple and the fieldfare isn't interested in the mealworms. It is even more intolerant of a female blackbird that flies in and lands some distance away; the fieldfare dashes over the snow at the new arrival, evidently identifying the bird as a potential threat to its apple. The blackbird is quickly seen off, and the fieldfare returns to its bounty.

At the feeders a great spotted woodpecker causes consternation by flying into the goat willow tree and then, after a quick look about, dropping down on to the fat ball feeder, displacing a group of five long-tailed tits that had been busily feeding away at it. The delicate feeding of the tits is replaced by the hacking of the woodpecker as it pecks a chunk of fat off one of the balls, scattering crumbs to the floor below, where I am sure the dunnock gratefully receives them. The woodpecker swallows the chunk and then, rearranging its position, grasping the metal cage of the feeder with its specialised feet, it chisels off another lump. This time, though, it flies off with its prize, its black and white plumage bouncing through the sky as it exits. A few seconds later, the tiny bundles of feather and long tails that are the long-tailed tits return to continue their more refined and delicate feeding.

The continuous traffic at the seed feeders has emptied them, so out I head to top them back up again. The fieldfare has to yield to me, hopping off into the protection of the pyracantha, but amazingly it doesn't fly; it sits within the thorny fortress whilst I pass by. I don't think I have ever been so close to a fieldfare before. I look down at the apple and laugh to myself as I look at the circle of uneaten mealworms that radiate out from the spot where the thrush has been sitting; all around them the snow is pecked and disturbed, and fragments of the brown larvae lie scattered about it, but the circle of untouched larvae is pristine, protected by a fieldfare forcefield.

Feeders topped up and mealworms scattered – this time in another, less protected, spot – I return inside and before I get back to my observation the fieldfare is already out of the hedge and settling in next to the apple. After a few more minutes it decides that it is hungry again, once more pecking hard at the fruit, breaking small pieces off that it readily swallows, then it settles down alongside it in quiet repose once again.

I don't know how long I spend watching all this avian activity; time doesn't matter. The amount of food that I have put out in the last few hours has a financial cost, but who cares? I see it more as an investment, an investment in my own well-being. The reward I get from watching all of this activity, the happiness I feel, is utterly priceless.

Seasonal awakenings

Following the road as it winds itself along the valley, mirroring the meandering river beside it, you cannot fail to notice the abundance of catkins dangling from the roadside hazels, adorning the tree's bare stems with the promise of new life. These are the proverbial lambtails of late winter, the male flowers that have responded to an increase in sunshine by suddenly elongating and opening up in what appears to be a coordinated effort. Absolutely every hazel along the few miles of road along which we are travelling has joined in the display.

Hazel, like many trees in Britain, produces both male and female flowers, both of which occur on the same branch. But whilst the male flowers, or catkins, are readily noticeable, the female ones are not; they are more bud-like, and only with a close-up view can you discern the 2-millimetre red stamens that protrude from their end like

Hazel catkins open up and dangle like the proverbial lamb's tails as winter nears its end.

a small tuft. They might not be showy, and are impossible to spot from the road, but it is these that will become the hazelnuts of next autumn, providing a feast for birds and mammals alike. The hazel produces its flowers before it bursts into leaf, a strategy that allows free passage of the windborne pollen from the catkins of neighbouring trees to the female flowers. It is only after this has happened that the leaf buds will begin to swell, turning the winter scene of brown poles into a veritable green curtain.

In some places the poles and their catkins are obscured by tangled masses of old man's beard, traveller's joy, bringing joy to us travellers as we drive along the winding roads. This is our wild clematis, a native relative of the showy climbers that some of us have in our gardens; the beards that are so noticeable now are the bunched-together fluffy appendages of the seeds that have ripened over the winter and are now ready to drop from the plant. The beardy wisps will catch the air currents, allowing the seeds to be carried along by the vagaries of the air; it is a random distribution of the seed – much will fall in unsuitable locations – but a small few will be more fortunate, finding that elusive goldilocks spot that is just right.

The hazel's catkins and the clematis's beards are two indicators that all is not as dormant as it might seem in the winter countryside. Winter is often referred to as the dormant season, a time when everything sleeps; but if you look closely you can see that many species are in fact active, albeit subtly, quietly preparing for the coming of the longer days and warmer temperatures of the spring. The hazel is a tree that is flowering; others are swelling their leaf buds; plants like the clematis are ensuring their seeds are dispersed at the most propitious time for them; and if you look carefully you may find a

Seasonality

158

dandelion or two sprouting fresh leaves. Birds too are slowly gearing up. For some, that means feeding voraciously on things like ivy berries, garnering as many calories as they can ahead of their migration back to their breeding grounds. For birds that stay all year, they too start to get prepared. Last year's young male blackbird is now firmly established in the garden, looking great in his new adult plumage; he is busy chasing off others from the garden that he feels is his, jealously guarding his resource of mealworm-providing humans.

Mistle thrushes are singing from the tops of the trees again, nuthatches wolf-whistle loudly on clear mornings, and the volume of the house sparrows has gone up several notches as the males start to regain their breeding plumage. Other noises can be heard; on damp nights the handful of frogs that stay resident in the pond all year around are already croaking. It is not the full chorus just yet, but that isn't far away, and soon the pond will be the setting for nights of frantic spawning and clasping.

With the breeding season in mind, some birds have already started visiting the nest boxes in the garden. A nuthatch, quite probably the one that has been whistling loudly, has already been pecking at the entrance hole of one of them, blue tits have taken to popping in and out of the box they used last year; at first they are probably looking for food, invertebrates tucked away in the shelter of the wooden box, but the visits become more regular and their tolerance of other blue tits in the box's vicinity has waned somewhat. The robin, in between singing its beautiful song, has also started frequenting the open-fronted robin box on the wall, jumping into it before hopping out and sitting on the roof, looking all around the box as if checking out the neighbourhood. Winter may be quieter than other seasons of the year, but its dormancy is a light one.

The edgy seaside

Rooks rumble their way into my consciousness with their raucous calls as a new February day dawns. I lie there in bed listening to them starting their day whilst I put off mine a bit longer. Rooks have such a variety of calls – high-pitched, low-pitched, drawn-out or abrupt – and there is a real vocabulary going on as they leave the safe procerity of the trees that form a small rookery in the heart of the village. They head off to the fields whilst I stay wrapped up in the warmth of my bed. As their calls fade into the distance a robin sings sweetly from the hawthorn right outside the window in a complete contrast to the rooks, but the message is the same: the day has begun.

As I fill the seed feeders the sky above me is full of noisy corvids. Jackdaws have joined the rooks, and the two are wheeling about the skyscape, one moment forming swirling chaotic corvid masses, the next flying in orderly formation. The sound is incredible, beautiful even. I stand for several minutes watching and listening to the happenings above me until I notice a coal tit sitting in one of the roses a few feet away, waiting patiently for me to leave the seed feeders it so desperately wants to get to.

At the bottom of the steps, a frog sits motionless on the concrete, its damp skin glistening, I carefully walk by it and head over to the pond. It has been a busy night by the looks of it; the pond weed looks unkempt, dragged strands of it littering the surface, a sure sign of lots of froggy activity. There are several frogs watching me warily, their heads just above the water's surface; there is no spawn to be seen yet, but the frogs are gearing up. It won't be long.

I head for the coast, to the town I grew up in, combining the son's duty with a bit of bird-watching along the way. It is probably my last chance this winter to catch up with a bird that will soon be departing for its breeding grounds far away to the north. The sea is grey and heavy; there is a swell driving the incoming tide, creating some classic-looking foamy waves. It looks perfect as I walk down the sea front, walking past the sandy beach to where the waves will be crashing into rocks by the old slipway.

I see them as soon as I can see the slipway: three stocky waders rapidly moving about the rocks as the waves break over them, hoping to snatch a crustacean that may have been dislodged by the crashing force of the wave. As the wave recedes one of them dashes in after it, aiming for a bladderwrack-wrapped rock, hoping to winkle out a winkle that has suddenly been exposed by the movement of the sea. Purple sandpipers are birds that really do live on the edge, eking out their living in the margin between land and sea. Not for them the quiet life of the mudflats on the estuary just a few hundred yards away: these birds are the ultimate surf-scurrying scuttlers.

Purple sandpipers look like darker, heavier versions of dunlin, their close relatives, but are much scarcer in numbers, with only around 13,000 purple sandpipers wintering with us. Dunlin, on the other hand, winter in UK estuaries in their hundreds of thousands.[103] This makes the purple sandpiper a bit of a tick for bird watchers, a bird that many seek out – and sure enough a couple of other binocular-wielding people are standing further along the seafront pavement, studying the birds as they dash in and out of the surf. I watch the waders for a few more minutes. They are completely wrapped up in what they are doing, completely focused on the waves of churned-up salt water, and completely ignoring the waves of people walking busily by just a few metres away. There is something hypnotic about the birds' movements, back and forth with the waves, running on their bright orange legs. For me it's very relaxing.

Further out, the fast-blurring wings of a red-breasted merganser catch the eye, its neck and head stretched out, pointing the way as the bird flies low over the water heading towards the mouth of the estuary. Above it herring gulls wheel over the sea, turning into the breeze and riding the lift, a laid-back flight that perfectly counterpoints the hectic action of the merganser. The purple sandpipers are still scuttling in and out of the surf, the two birdwatchers are still watching them, and I drift back along the seafront as the sun breaks through the cloud.

Up by the old inshore lifeboat station a small bird is sitting on the apex of a wooden shed situated at the back of a classic seaside café. It is a brown bird – not much to look at to be honest; it doesn't have the cachet that the purple sandpiper has – and as I look about me I notice that I am the only person paying it any attention. But like the orange-

Seasonality

---

103 Population data for both species taken from the BTO website.

legged wader I was watching a few moments ago, this is a bird of the coastal margin, albeit a coastal margin that is a bit higher up the beach.

Our three breeding pipits are birds with names that are a fair guide as to where you should be looking for them. The meadow pipit does indeed like grassy areas, and the tree pipit likes nothing better than a tree to land in after its descending-song flight, but the rock pipit is a bit more specialised than its name indicates. It does like rocks, but it likes them to be at the seaside. If you look at a distribution map of this pipit you will see that it forms a border all around the coasts of Great Britain and Ireland. It is not as numerous as the other two breeding pipits: there are only around 36,000 pairs of rock pipits distributed around the coast of Britain, compared to the 105,000 pairs of tree pipits that breed here in the spring and summer, and the 2.5 million of the much more ubiquitous meadow pipit – but if you are at the seaside, particularly a rocky one, you are likely to find one if you look.

At this time of year they can be found away from their usual rockier haunts. This bird is several hundred metres away from where I will see it in the spring and summer, when it breeds in the rocks of the slowly collapsing cliffs that form the eastern end of the beach. With no breeding tie, it has left the cliff section of the sea front and is now currently surveying the flatter section of the shore from its elevated wooden shed of a perch: a miniature substitute cliff perhaps? It drops down from its lookout, landing on the beach in amongst a strandline deposited by a far higher tide than today's; it finds something to eat in amongst the dried-out seaweed and driftwood, and snaffles it down quickly before moving onwards along the line of sea-dumped debris. I watch it heading off on its beachcombing mission, walking along, occasionally stopping to poke at something with its bill or to flip over a promising bit of seaweed; at one point it flips up into the air and snatches a flying insect it has disturbed.

Pipits are great little birds, always busy, and this one is no exception as it hurries along the line of flotsam on the beach before it is rudely interrupted by a dog chasing a tennis ball. The bird decides that it is time to return to the safety of the wooden shed cliff I first saw it on, and once there it perches in the same spot as before, basking in the sunlight. The scattering of droppings on the roof of the shed imply that this is a favourite spot of this coast-loving, edge-living bird.

The cold returns

As February arrives so does another period of cold weather: a high-pressure system is fixed over Scandinavia, funnelling easterly winds across Britain, lowering temperatures throughout, even here in the South West. The air is dry and crystal clear, but the temperature is freezing, staying around zero during the day and plummeting below once darkness arrives. A walk to the local shop in the morning is approached like a polar expedition: multiple layers, gloves and hat are all donned before I step out into the cold morning air.

The dryness of the air and the accompanying wind mean that there is no frost on the grass, but the sting of the temperature is plain to see: the grass sits all pinched and collapsed along the verge, and even the leaves of the bramble hang limply, beaten into submission by the cold. Normally this stretch of road, with its unkempt margins merging into a bramble and blackthorn scrub, are full of small birds, but this morning there is nothing moving, nothing calling. It is eerily silent as I walk along. I wonder where the birds have gone, where they have moved to, where they are taking shelter and finding food within their landscape that they know intimately. The return journey from the shop, walking directly into the wind, prickles my exposed face with its harshness, and by the time I get home my face is red. It is no wonder that the birds have sought a more sheltered site.

Out in the garden, every water source is frozen hard, even around the exposed pebbles in the pond which normally help to retain a bit of liquid water. I carefully break the ice around the pebbles to create some open water, a resource even more precious for birds than food on a morning like this. Birds feeding on the dry diet of seeds in our feeders need access to water. Without it they will die. Even before I am back in the house, the sparrows that were watching me from the bramble honeysuckle tangle in which they spend so much time have dropped down to the pond to drink.

A look out the window reveals two contrasting scenes; the first is a little wren, puffed up like a ball, using its feathers to trap an insulating layer of air around its tiny body. The word 'ball' is a good analogy for this bird, as it seems to bounce and roll along the garden, searching every part of it for food, never seeming to stop for a moment. A winter avian scene. But the other scene, despite the bitterness of the weather, speaks more of the season to come than of the present. A wood pigeon, plump and proud-looking, lands on the patio, its plumage a beautiful mix of soft greys. After a moment of looking around, it waddles around sedately, pecking at strands of vegetation and pulling at any that look promising, before it finally settles on a twig lying wind-stranded on the concrete. It picks it up in its bill and seems to almost size it up before up it flies onto the rounded burred ends of the pollarded willow in the upper garden. It sits there momentarily, holding its nest material aloft, before it flies into the clematis-tangled branches of the top hawthorn that grows on our boundary. The air may be bitterly cold, and other birds may be struggling to survive this winter weather, but the wood pigeon is busy nest-building.

Wood pigeons don't follow the typical pattern of birds nesting in Britain. Most birds have a strict period in which they breed, invariably in the spring, but the wood pigeon can breed all year around if food sources are abundant enough. I've seen them sitting on eggs in December, so seeing one starting to build a nest in February doesn't come as too much of a surprise. The British Trust for Ornithology's nest record scheme has records for the first eggs being laid anywhere from 22 February to 20 August;[104] the birds obviously don't allow the cold weather to interfere with their plans.

The cold blast of air that we are subject to changes the birding in the garden. Species we don't normally get here appear, allowing us to watch them at close quarters; one of these is the bullfinch. These stout little finches are beautiful birds, a mix of pink, grey and

104 BTO BirdFacts, Woodpigeon.

A female bullfinch in one of the young Devon whitebeams in the garden.

black. These were the cover birds of the first bird book I ever owned, the *Ladybird Book of Garden Birds*,[105] given to me at a young age. I used to look covetously at those birds on the cover, as bullfinches weren't birds that I saw as a child, and that lack of actually seeing them combined with them gracing the cover of my only bird book led to them achieving an almost mythical status in my young mind.

They are regulars around the village, a typical mid-Devon settlement with lots of scattered apple trees, a remnant of the self-sufficiency that rural villages once had. Bullfinches love apple trees, but apple tree owners don't necessarily love bullfinches. They have an older, alternative name, bud bird, and it is a good name for them: bullfinches do indeed like to eat buds, and they have a preference in the spring for the buds and young shoots of fruit trees such as the apple, the pear and the plum, and it is this predilection that has brought them into conflict with us in the past. It is still possible to apply for a licence to kill them to prevent damage to fruit trees.

But for me, seeing bullfinches is always a delight, bringing back those memories from childhood, and to get them in the garden is an added thrill. But these winter visitors to our garden aren't after the buds on our apple tree; they don't even perch in it. I am not entirely sure what they are after, but I think they are gleaning aphids. In freezing cold

105 Published in 1967. I still have it.

weather, birds have no choice but to adapt their diet, to take advantage of food sources they might not normally exploit.

The bullfinch that is visiting the garden in this spate of cold weather is a female; she is less pink than the male, but is still a spectacular bird. She comes in late in the afternoon when the light is already falling away, and she always heads to the bramble and honeysuckle tangle so favoured by the sparrows. Unlike the noisy boisterous sparrows, though, she doesn't enter into the tangle; she flies around its edge with incredibly rapid wing beats. She is basically hovering, but in a laborious way, her wings no more than a hectic blur to my eyes as I watch her from the far end of the patio. I stand there wrapped up in my layers, trying to work out what it is she is doing every afternoon.

Her wings flapping furiously, she elongates her body and, using her chubby black bill, she seems to be very carefully picking something off the confused entanglement of honeysuckle stems that weave their way through the bramble. Occasionally she will perch on a bramble twig and lean forward towards a honeysuckle stem, very delicately picking something off it with her heavy, short bill that is clearly not adapted for such a feeding technique. She feeds in this manner for several minutes and then she's away. I only ever see this behaviour in really cold weather, and can only surmise that she is feeding on aphids or something very similar. One thing I am certain of, though, is that when the promised low pressure arrives later in the week, bringing with it warm south-westerly air, she will stop her late afternoon visits to the garden.

The last week of February begins with some much-needed sunshine and real warmth. Everything responds: suddenly there are queen bumblebees bumbling along in the sunshine, finding succour in the primroses in the garden; several honeybees are also buzzing about, visiting the snowdrops that have been blooming unattended for a couple of weeks; but the biggest response is a vocal one. A male great tit, his black stripe broadening across his belly, is in the hawthorn above the highest bird box, proclaiming 'Teacher – Teacher' to all that will listen. The pair of blue tits who have been assiduously keeping an eye on the box since the turn of the year are scolding away at him with concern.

Our male blackbird is still in soft voice mode, sitting outside the kitchen window on his perch and quietly testing his song, but others are not so shy. A song thrush is singing beautifully further off, repeating its variations loudly, beautifully. Bright male greenfinches trill excitedly, and the sparrows are busy being noisy and gathering nest material, arguing over stray pigeon feathers and wispy twigs, whilst the male dunnocks are not only singing but have even started their distinctive wing-flicking display, whirring their wings at one another as if in some bizarre armpit-comparison ritual. The wren and robin are still singing, but their songs have become more strident and more regular, performed from perches where they can be seen and heard. The nuthatch, when not dashing into the feeders at breakneck speed, is loudly whistling his song, the sound resounding around the gardens. Even a raptor feels moved to be heard: overhead in the blue sky, a buzzard is circling and calling out as it screws itself upwards.

It is that time of year when winter starts to loosen its grip, to relax its hold. But spring isn't quite ready; the clear blue sun-filled sky of the day will lead to the temperatures dropping rapidly later, bringing with it a frost to nip the unwary. Just a few weeks ago the frogs were busy in the pond, but since the bitterly cold snap there has been no activity, and even though the weather is now warming up nicely in the daytime the amphibians are not to be lured back into action. Frogs can spawn early, but if the spawn gets iced into frozen water much of it will perish before it has even begun. For the frogs it pays to be cautious. Even at the end of February, all is quiet in the pond for now.

Daffodils

The late February sunshine didn't last long. The air temperature has gone up and the nights are once again frost-free, but the blue sky has been replaced with a leaden grey. I head out along the lanes that radiate out from the village, walking over the wet tarmac and looking forward to the return of the sun. Yellow-headed fugitives bring a splash of much-needed colour to the verges and hedge banks on this dull afternoon. Daffodils,

Daffodils beneath the ragged remnants of what could be a vibrant hedgerow.

smuggled out from their garden confines, dot the lanes. They shouldn't be here. They are not the wild daffodils of Wordsworth's immortal words, but manipulated garden centre varieties that have no place in the wider countryside. They are a garden escape, not a natural wonder. But then, when I look at their setting below the skeletal remains of what we optimistically call hedges when in fact they are no more than flailed torn ragged sticks, I wonder if I am being disingenuous with my scorn. From an aesthetic point of view, the introduced daffodils are far more attractive than our 'carefully managed' hedgerows.

Our countryside is not natural; there is virtually nowhere in Britain that hasn't been radically altered by humans. Farmland in particular is a completely artificial landscape. The field on the other side of the so-called hedge under which these yellow flowers are growing is used to grow maize, a plant that originated in the Americas and has nothing to do with European flora, let alone British. I look at the daffodils, their stalks moving in the breeze, their beautiful yellow flowers nodding along in time with the rhythm of the wind; they are lovely. I decide my scorn is misplaced in this highly managed landscape. The flowers are like miniature suns, burning bright in the dwindling light.

Off in the background, framing the scene, the high hills of north Dartmoor are looking dark and foreboding; the moorland has been coloured by the sky's mood. High Willhays and Yes Tor are sitting beneath a large hulking mass of dark grey cloud, an angry sky full of the promise of precipitation. A storm is coming. A straggly line of lesser black-backed gulls flies high above the mid-Devon plain and a buzzard soars on an uplift of air, but other than that the darkening sky is empty. The breeze is stiffening, gathering momentum; the rain in those dark grey clouds on the horizon will be here soon. The daffodils are nodding more vigorously now. It is a sign for me to head for home.

Looking out of the bedroom window later in the day, I watch the storm unleash its anger. Overhead the sky is a furious dark grey from horizon to horizon; the trees that I can see are all bending in the relentless raging wind, the fierceness of it generating gusts that test the trees to the extreme, threatening to rend them into no more than shattered firewood. Rain lashes down, an unceasing downpour as relentless as the wind. The storm bites, and bites hard – and through it all, through the seething tumult, an unseen robin sings continuously. The weather might not acknowledge it, but the bird knows. The seasons of the year roll on regardless: an endless cycle that dictates the rhythm of life. Spring is coming.

Appendix:
Species mentioned in the text

It is only when you come to list the names of species that you realise how complicated names can be! To avoid any confusion and complication, I have chosen to use the names by which each species is commonly known in the UK. Many species, especially birds, are often listed in guides with a more international name in brackets – for example, the avocet is often listed as (pied) avocet – but for the purpose of this book I have dropped all such bracketed names. Of course, it goes without saying that any mistakes in these lists will be mine alone.

Birds

Avocet	*Recurvirostra avosetta*
Barn Owl	*Tyto alba*
Bar-tailed Godwit	*Limosa lapponica*
Blackbird	*Turdus merula*
Blackcap	*Sylvia atricapilla*
Black-tailed Godwit	*Limosa limosa*
Blue Tit	*Cyanistes caeruleus*
Brambling	*Fringilla montifringilla*
Brent Goose	*Branta bernicla*
Bullfinch	*Pyrrhula pyrrhula*
Buzzard	*Buteo buteo*
Canada Goose	*Branta canadensis*
Carrion Crow	*Corvus corone*
Chaffinch	*Fringilla coelebs*
Chiffchaff	*Phylloscopus collybita*
Coal Tit	*Periparus ater*
Cormorant	*Phalacrocorax carbo*
Curlew	*Numenius arquata*
Dipper	*Cinclus cinclus*
Dodo	*Raphus cucullatus*

Dunlin	*Calidris alpina*
Dunnock	*Prunella modularis*
Feral/Domestic Pigeon	*Columba livia domestica*
Fieldfare	*Turdus pilaris*
Gadwall	*Anas strepera*
Gannet	*Morus bassanus*
Goldcrest	*Regulus regulus*
Goldfinch	*Carduelis carduelis*
Great Black-backed Gull	*Larus marinus*
Great Spotted Woodpecker	*Dendrocopos major*
Great Tit	*Parus major*
Green Sandpiper	*Tringa ochropus*
Green Woodpecker	*Picus viridis*
Greenfinch	*Chloris chloris*
Greenshank	*Tringa nebularia*
Grey Heron	*Ardea cinerea*
Grey Wagtail	*Motacilla cinerea*
Greylag Goose	*Anser anser*
Hawfinch	*Coccothraustes coccothraustes*
Herring Gull	*Larus argentatus*
Hobby	*Falco subbuteo*
House Martin	*Delichon urbicum*
House Sparrow	*Passer domesticus*
Jackdaw	*Corvus monedula*
Jay	*Garrulus glandarius*
Kestrel	*Falco tinnunculus*
Kingfisher	*Alcedo atthis*
Lapwing	*Vanellus vanellus*
Lesser Black-backed Gull	*Larus fuscus*
Lesser Redpoll	*Acanthis cabaret*
Linnet	*Carduelis cannabina*
Little Egret	*Egretta garzetta*
Long-tailed Tit	*Aegithalos caudatus*
Mallard	*Anas platyrhynchos*
Meadow Pipit	*Anthus pratensis*
Mistle Thrush	*Turdus viscivorus*
Moorhen	*Gallinula chloropus*
Nightjar	*Caprimulgus europaeus*
Nuthatch	*Sitta europaea*
Oystercatcher	*Haematopus ostralegus*
Passenger Pigeon	*Ectopistes migratorius*
Peregrine	*Falco peregrinus*
Pied Flycatcher	*Ficedula hypoleuca*
Pied Wagtail	*Motacilla alba yarrellii*
Pintail	*Anas acuta*
Pochard	*Aythya ferina*

Purple Sandpiper	*Calidris maritima*
Raven	*Corvus corax*
Razorbill	*Alca torda*
Red-breasted Merganser	*Mergus serrator*
Redshank	*Tringa totanus*
Redwing	*Turdus iliacus*
Ring Ouzel	*Turdus torquatus*
Robin	*Erithacus rubecula*
Rock Pipit	*Anthus petrosus*
Rook	*Corvus frugilegus*
Ruff	*Philomachus pugnax*
Shag	*Phalacrocorax aristotelis*
Shoveler	*Anas clypeata*
Siskin	*Carduelis spinus*
Skylark	*Alauda arvensis*
Snipe	*Gallinago gallinago*
Song Thrush	*Turdus philomelos*
Sparrowhawk	*Accipiter nisus*
Spotted Flycatcher	*Muscicapa striata*
Spotted Redshank	*Tringa erythropus*
Starling	*Sturnus vulgaris*
Stonechat	*Saxicola torquatus*
Swallow	*Hirundo rustica*
Swift	*Apus apus*
Tawny Owl	*Strix aluco*
Teal	*Anas crecca*
Tree Pipit	*Anthus trivialis*
Treecreeper	*Certhia familiaris*
Tufted Duck	*Aythya fuligula*
Turtle Dove	*Streptopelia turtur*
Water Rail	*Rallus aquaticus*
Wheatear	*Oenanthe oenanthe*
Whimbrel	*Numenius phaeopus*
Whitethroat	*Sylvia communis*
Wigeon	*Anas penelope*
Willow Warbler	*Phylloscopus trochilus*
Wood Pigeon	*Columba polumbus*
Wood Warbler	*Phylloscopus sibilatrix*
Woodcock	*Scolopax rusticola*
Wren	*Troglodytes troglodytes*
Yellowhammer	*Emberiza citrinella*

Fungi

Amethyst Deceiver	*Laccaria amethystina*
Angel's Bonnet	*Mycena arcangeliana*

Aniseed Funnel	*Clitocybe odora*
Cep	*Boletus edulis*
Death Cap	*Amanita phalloides*
Dutch Elm Disease Fungus	*Ophiostoma novo-ulmi*
Giant Polypore	*Meripilus giganteus*
Ochre Brittlegill	*Russula ochroleuca*
Old Man of the Woods	*Strobilomyces strobilaceus*
Panther Cap	*Amanita pantherina*
Pink Disco	*Aleurodiscus wakefieldiae*
Poison Pie	*Hebeloma crustuliniforme*
Salmon Salad	*Guepinia helvelloides*
Shooting Star	*Sphaerobolus stellatus*
Slippery Jack	*Suillus luteus*
Tiger's Eye	*Coltricia perennis*
Wood Hedgehog	*Hydnum repandum*
Zoned Tooth	*Hydnellum concrescens*

Herptiles

Adder	*Vipera berus*
Barred Grass Snake	*Natrix helvetica*
Common Frog	*Rana temporaria*
Palmate Newt	*Lissotriton helveticus*
Slow Worm	*Anguis fragilis*
Smooth Snake	*Coronella austriaca*

Invertebrates

Banded Agrion	*Agrion splendens*
Black Bean Aphid	*Aphis fabae*
Black Garden Ant	*Lasius niger*
Bramble Leaf Miner Moth	*Stigmella aurella*
Brimstone Butterfly	*Gonepteryx rhamni*
Brimstone Moth	*Opisthograptis luteolata*
Comma	*Polygonia c-album*
Common Marbled Carpet	*Dysstroma truncata*
Common Wasp	*Vespula vulgaris*
Crab Spider	*Misumena vatia*
Cranefly	*Tipulidae spp*
Daddy Long-legs Spider	*Pholcus phalangioides*
Early Bumblebee	*Bombus pratorum*
Emperor Dragonfly	*Anax imperator*
Garden Spider	*Araneus diadematus*
German Wasp	*Vespula germanica*
Gnat/Mosquito	*Culex & Aedes spp*
Golden-ringed Dragonfly	*Cordulegaster boltonii*

Hornet Clearwing	*Sesia apiformis*
Hornet Mimic Hoverfly	*Volucella zonaria*
Hornet	*Vespa crabro*
House Spider	*Tegenaria domestica*
Hoverfly	*Syrphidae spp*
Ivy Bee	*Colletes hederae*
Magpie Moth	*Abraxas grossulariata*
Meadow Brown	*Maniola jurtina*
Orange-tip	*Anthocharis cardamines*
Painted Lady	*Vanessa cardui*
Peacock Butterfly	*Aglais io*
Privet Hawkmoth	*Sphinx ligustri*
Red Admiral	*Vanessa atalanta*
Red Mason Bee	*Osmia bicornis*
Scalloped Hazel	*Odontopera bidentata*
Silver Y Moth	*Autographa gamma*
Silver-Ground Carpet	*Xanthorhoe montanata*
Silver-washed Fritillary	*Argynnis paphia*
Small Tortoiseshell	*Aglais urticae*
Solitary Wasp	*Sapyga quinquepunctata*
Speckled Wood	*Pararge aegeria*
Woodlouse Spider	*Dysdera crocata*
Woodlouse	*Oniscidea spp*

Mammals

Badger	*Meles meles*
Bank Vole	*Myodes glareolus*
Black Rat	*Rattus rattus*
Brown Rat	*Rattus norvegicus*
Common Dormouse	*Muscardinus avellanarius*
Common Shrew	*Sorex araneus*
Fallow Deer	*Dama dama*
Field Vole	*Microtus agrestis*
Fox	*Vulpes vulpes*
Grey Squirrel	*Sciurus carolinensis*
Hedgehog	*Erinaceus europaeus*
Lynx	*Lynx lynx*
Polecat	*Mustela putorius*
Rabbit	*Oryctolagus cuniculus*
Red Deer	*Cervus elaphus*
Roe Deer	*Capreolus capreolus*
Sika Deer	*Cervus nippon*
Stoat	*Mustela erminea*
Weasel	*Mustela nivalis*
Wild Boar	*Sus scrofa*

| Wolf | Canis lupus |
| Wood Mouse | Apodemus sylvaticus |

Plants

Bilberry	Vaccinium myrtillus
Bluebell	Hyacinthoides non-scripta
Borage	Borago officinalis
Bracken	Pteridium aquilinum
Bramble	Rubus agg
Buddleia	Buddleja davidii
Cherry Laurel	Prunus laurocerasus
Cosmos	Cosmos spp
Cow Parsley	Anthriscus sylvestris
Daffodil	Narcissus spp
Dandelion	Taraxacum officinale
Dog's Mercury	Mercurialis perennis
Garlic Mustard	Alliaria petiolata
Greater Stitchwort	Rabelera holostea
Heather	Calluna vulgaris
Honeysuckle	Lonicera periclymenum
Ivy	Hedera helix
Lungwort	Pulmonaria officinalis
Marjoram	Origanum vulgare
Primrose	Primula vulgaris
Pyracantha	Pyracantha rogersiana
Rhododendron	Rhododendron ponticum
St. John's Wort	Hypericum spp
Traveller's Joy	Clematis vitalba
Western Gorse	Ulex gallii

Trees

Alder Buckthorn	Frangula alnus
Blackthorn	Prunus spinosa
Common Alder	Alnus glutinosa
Common Ash	Fraxinus excelsior
Common Beech	Fagus sylvatica
Common Hawthorn	Crataegus monogyna
Common Hazel	Corylus avellana
Common Holly	Ilex aquifolium
Common Hornbeam	Carpinus betulus
Common Lime	Tilia x europaea
Common Rowan	Sorbus aucuparia
Common Yew	Taxus baccata
Devon Whitebeam	Karpatiosorbus devoniensis

Douglas Fir	*Pseudotsuga menziesii*
Downy Birch	*Betula pubescens*
Field Elm	*Ulmus minor*
Field Maple	*Acer campestre*
Goat Willow	*Salix caprea*
Guelder Rose	*Viburnum opulus*
No Parking Whitebeam	*Karpatiosorbus admonitor*
Pedunculate Oak	*Quercus robur*
Scots Pine	*Pinus sylvestris*
Sessile Oak	*Quercus petraea*
Silver Birch	*Betula pendula*
Sitka Spruce	*Picea sitchensis*
Smoke-bush	*Cotinus coggygria*
Spindle	*Euonymus europaeus*
Sweet Chestnut	*Castanea sativa*
Sweet Gum	*Liquidambar styraciflua*
Sycamore	*Acer pseudoplatanus*
Wayfaring Tree	*Viburnum lantana*

Strictly speaking, trees are of course just plants, and there are no hard and fast rules for what makes a tree a tree, so the above list is my personal choice from the plants listed in this book. Trees are just a human concept, a disparate collection of plants that we have decided, in our wisdom, to lump together under one word without any biological justification whatsoever. A Giant Redwood and a Dwarf Birch may be what we call trees, but they are as closely related to one another as we are to a halibut. Gorse has more wood in it than a Palm on the seafront of Torquay, but gorse is a bush and the palm is a tree … There is no unifying factor that makes a tree a tree. You could make an argument for both Rhododendron and Cherry Laurel to be included in this list as opposed to the more general plant list, but I decided that for the purpose of this book they fitted better in there.